Beyond
Nuclear Deterrence

Beyond Nuclear Deterrence

Transforming the U.S.– Russian Equation

Alexei Arbatov
Vladimir Dvorkin

with
Vladimir Evseev

Foreword by John D. Steinbruner

CARNEGIE ENDOWMENT FOR INTERNATIONAL PEACE
Washington, D.C.

Carnegie Endowment for International Peace
1779 Massachusetts Avenue, N.W., Washington, D.C. 20036
202-483-7600, Fax 202-483-1840
www.CarnegieEndowment.org

The Carnegie Endowment for International Peace normally does not take institutional positions on public policy issues; the views and recommendations presented in this publication do not necessarily represent the views of the Carnegie Endowment, its officers, staff, or trustees.

A previous version of this work was published as *Revising Nuclear Deterrence* as part of the Advanced Methods of Cooperative Security Program at the Center for International and Security Studies at Maryland (November 2005).

To order, contact:
Hopkins Fulfillment Service
P.O. Box 50370, Baltimore, MD 21211-4370
1-800-537-5487 or 1-410-516-6956
Fax 1-410-516-6998

Composition by Stephen McDougal
Printed by Automated Graphics Systems

Library of Congress Cataloging-in-Publication data

Arbatov, Aleksei Georgievich.
   Beyond nuclear deterrence : transforming the U.S.-Russian equation /
Alexei Arbatov, Vladimir Dvorkin, with Vladimir Evseev.
      p. cm.
   Summary: "Arbatov and Dvorkin assess the history of deterrence between
the Soviet Union and the U.S. and its evolution through the Cold War. The
two countries need to take steps to remove mutual nuclear deterrence as the
foundation of their strategic relationship and implement changes that can be
exported internationally"—Provided by publisher.
   Includes bibliographical references and index.
   ISBN-13: 978-0-87003-226-4 (pbk.)
   ISBN-10: 0-87003-226-7 (pbk.)
   ISBN-13: 978-0-87003-227-1 (hardcover)
   ISBN-10: 0-87003-227-5 (hardcover)
   1. Nuclear arms control—United States. 2. Nuclear arms control—Russia
(Federation) 3. Security, International. I. Dvorkin, Vladimir. II. Evseev,
Vladimir. III. Title.

   JZ5665.A73 2006
   355.02'17—dc22   2006014845

11 10 09 08 07 06   1 2 3 4 5   1st Printing 2006

Contents

Foreword

When the Russian Federation emerged from the dissolution of the Soviet Union as the principal successor state, it immediately encountered a security burden that was at the outset and still remains the most demanding in the world. Russia absorbed the bulk of the Soviet military establishment, including all of its nuclear weapons, about half of its conventional munitions, some 75 percent of its territory, and its entire legacy of active confrontation with the U.S. alliance system. It thereby acquired responsibility for preserving the global deterrent balance while also defending a truncated territory highly exposed to violent political grievances, especially along its lengthy southern borders. The assets Russia inherited were neither adequate nor appropriate for performing the required security missions. The sheer size of the nuclear arsenal appeared to guarantee the preservation of deterrence, no longer considered to be politically contested, but the residual conventional forces could not credibly prevent air incursion in the West or ground incursion in the East. Nor could they ensure control of civil insurgencies. Moreover, the economic base of the new federation was not sufficient to remove those deficiencies, even with a dedicated effort to do so, and competing priorities of economic and social development precluded such an effort.

Russia's response to the inherited situation has been embedded in a general process of internal reform intended to establish a consensual political process and to align the economy with global market conditions. Investment in the military establishment has been sharply restricted, and economic development has concentrated heavily on a natural comparative advantage—oil and gas exports. The implicit security strategy is to rely for protection far more on political accommodation and economic engagement than on countervailing military capability. One can debate how much internal reform Russia has been able to accomplish in support of this strategy, but it is evident that a serious effort has been made. After a millennium of authoritarian rule, the Russian political system now confers authority through voting procedures, and after decades of isolation the economy is now intimately engaged in global markets. Russia can be fairly described as an emerging industrial democracy even though the term is seldom explicitly applied.

Nonetheless, despite extensive efforts to undertake internal transformation and external accommodation, Russia has not been relieved of the burdens of military confrontation, especially not by the United States, whose policy on that point is the one that most matters. Fifteen years after the Cold War was declared to have ended, the United States continues to preserve a massive, actively deployed deterrent capability directed against Russia. Thousands of nuclear weapons are continuously maintained on immediately available alert status able to undertake large scale attacks within a few hours. The practice is said to be justified by the traditional doctrine of assured retaliation, but it also could support the far more contentious doctrine of preemption. In addition NATO has extended its jurisdiction to the borders of Russia and thereby enhanced its formidable capacities for conventional air incursion. No direct antagonism is expressed, and U.S. political officials regularly assert that Russia is not considered a potential enemy. But it is a core principle of security policy that reliable protection must be based on capacity rather than declared intent, since the latter is more readily misrepresented or at any rate more rapidly changed. In terms of inherent military capacity and routine operational practice, the United States continues to impose relentless pressure on Russia.

In this book two of Russia's most thoughtful and most widely respected security specialists argue for more extensive security accommodation between their country and the United States, beginning with a transformation of the legacy deterrent relationship. They suggest that the predominant common interest in the new political situation is to establish more robust protection against the potential diversion or misuse of nuclear weapons—an interest that is seriously undermined by current operational practices and could only be achieved through direct collaboration. To establish the foundation for mutually beneficial collaboration, they argue for explicit termination of the deterrent policy, and they advance a series of specific recommendations as to how that could be accomplished. Those recommendations feature extensive reduction and deactivation of Russian and U.S. offensive forces, integration of the early warning systems, joint development and deployment of missile defense systems, and joint efforts to establish global stabilization measures. In the context of recent history and current policy, their argument might seem to be implausibly venturesome, but it is nonetheless rather compelling common sense. One can at least hope that common sense presented as lucidly and as judiciously as it is in this book by authors as highly regarded as Alexei Arbatov and Vladimir Dvorkin has some decent chance of prevailing in due course.

—John D. Steinbruner, Director,
Center for International and Security
Studies at Maryland (CISSM)

Acknowledgments

We are grateful to the Center for International and Security Studies at the University of Maryland (CISSM) for initiating this study on the past, present, and future of nuclear deterrence, and to the John D. and Catherine T. MacArthur Foundation for supporting that work. The Carnegie Endowment for International Peace also is deeply grateful to the MacArthur Foundation, the Carnegie Corporation of New York, and the Charles Stewart Mott Foundation for their support of the Moscow Center's nonproliferation work. Our special thanks go to John D. Steinbruner, who provided valuable intellectual guidance and comments on the subject of this book, and to Nancy Gallagher for organizing our efficient interaction during the whole research period. We also greatly appreciate the organizational help and support of the CISSM and Carnegie Moscow Center staff, as well as the comments and advice of all Russian and American experts who have read all or part of this book or have discussed with us its various details. At the same time, we, as the authors, bear full responsibility for the assumptions, theoretical analysis, and practical proposals of the study.

CHAPTER ONE

Introduction

The goal of *Beyond Nuclear Deterrence* is to elaborate on proposals that could help transform the current state of mutual nuclear deterrence, foremost between the two biggest
nuclear powers—Russia and the United States—into a new
mode of relations based on mutual management of nuclear
weapons balance and control over its impact on international
security. Transformation of this kind, beginning in a bilateral
format, will at some point have to embrace multilateral strategic relations among the five principal nuclear powers and the
new nuclear weapon states, as well as some aspects of the development, deployment, and use of conventional forces.

Even when dramatic changes occur in the political relations
between nuclear states that make them stop seeing each other
as adversaries, as with Russia and the United States following
the Cold War, these states' armed forces, and foremost their
nuclear forces, retain the powerful momentum of confrontation
and competition. These forces cannot adjust to new cooperative
political relations on their own without political and technical
efforts that are consistent, well designed, and bilateral.

Furthermore, newly emerging adversaries, contingencies, and
challenges brought about by nuclear proliferation and various

conflicts of national interests may destabilize strategic relations between the former enemies. The result can be increased tensions in their strategic policies, with highly detrimental political, military, and legal arms control consequences.

For example, the 2002 U.S. decision to test and deploy a strategic ballistic missile defense (BMD) system, allegedly designed to defend the United States from the new countries (that is, "rogue states") possessing ballistic missiles, and Washington's withdrawal from the 1972 Anti-Ballistic Missile (ABM) Treaty, made Russia place increased reliance on its offensive strategic nuclear force. Thus, Moscow extended the service lives of those of its heavy intercontinental ballistic missiles (ICBMs) equipped with multiple independently targeted reentry vehicles (MIRVs) and even purchased a few dozen MIRV missiles from Ukraine's stockpile. Also, as reported by President Vladimir Putin, Russia has accelerated development of a new strategic offensive weapon system fitted with a gliding and maneuvering reentry vehicle designed to penetrate "any BMD system." In keeping with post–Cold War sensitivities no specific opponent has been mentioned, but this new system can only be assumed to be intended to target the United States.

Russia reacted in a similar way to a new U.S. program of nuclear earth-penetrating warheads allegedly designed to destroy underground bunkers in terrorist-held areas and rogue states. Many Russians believe that this program is directed at Russia's own hardened sites. As Russia's defense minister, Sergei Ivanov, said, "Moscow is attentively tracking the developments in the U.S. strategic nuclear force. In particular, we are not indifferent to the U.S. programs of developing mini–nuclear weapons, for each new type of weapon adds up new elements to the general picture of global stability. We are to take it into account in our military planning."[1]

Since the end of the Cold War, nuclear deterrence between Russia and the United States has been receding into the background in terms of day-to-day foreign policy and official public relations. Although both countries retain thousands of nuclear warheads, they have ceased to be global rivals and the chances of a deliberate war between them have fallen close to zero.

Despite serious differences on some issues, such as Yugoslavia (1999), Iraq (2003), Russian domestic politics and their effect on elections in Ukraine (2004), the eastward expansion of the North Atlantic Treaty Organization (NATO, 1999 and 2003), and a growing U.S. presence in several of the former Soviet republics, Moscow and Washington are no longer the leaders of two coalitions of states and political-ideological movements that had made bipolarity the global norm in international relations for almost five decades. Their relations—despite continuous ups and downs, friction, disagreements, and mutual recrimination—include numerous and important areas of cooperation.

This cooperation has embraced various economic and political spheres, peacekeeping operations, resolution of regional conflicts, nonproliferation of weapons of mass destruction (WMD), the struggle against terrorism, joint ground and naval exercises, programs to secure and eliminate stockpiles of nuclear and chemical weapons, safe disposal of nuclear materials and decommissioned nuclear submarines, salvage operations at sea, and joint human space systems.

Since the early 1990s, the United States and Russia have halved their deployed strategic nuclear forces in terms of nuclear reentry vehicles (warheads) under the 1991 Strategic Arms Reduction Treaty (START I), and are expected to reduce them by another 60 percent by 2012 under the 2002 Strategic Offensive Reduction Treaty (SORT). Combined with cuts in both sides' tactical nuclear arms, the reductions will apparently amount to at least 80 percent over the twenty-year period since the early 1990s.

But there is also the other side of the coin. Unlike before, the United States, Russia, and some of the other great powers have openly or tacitly rejected the idea of nuclear disarmament as an indispensable, if abstract, condition of general security. Worse yet, as their official doctrines, arms programs, and military budgets indicate, they are dismantling the complex of central nuclear disarmament agreements to keep maximum freedom of action in technical development and plans for combat use of nuclear weapons. For instance, the George W. Bush administration does not consider it worthwhile even to discuss strategic nuclear reduction measures subsequent to SORT, and has rejected both the

ABM treaty and the Comprehensive Test-Ban Treaty of 1996. The administration has apparently also lost interest in the Fissile Material Cut-off Treaty, as well as universal measures to enhance the effectiveness of the Nuclear Non-Proliferation Treaty.

Moreover, Washington is now emphasizing the right to launch preemptive selective nuclear strikes, thereby promoting a doctrine of actual nuclear warfare rather than of traditional nuclear deterrence. A serious program, although not without disputes and setbacks, is now underway in the United States to develop advanced nuclear weapons allegedly designed to destroy hardened bunkers and other installations of rogue countries and terrorists with less fallout and collateral damage.

This example is being followed by Russia, although with some reservations and a variety of controversial official declarations. After a rather weak resistance, Moscow has resigned itself to the United States' current lack of interest in arms control treaties, and has demonstrated that it cannot oppose Washington effectively at the political, diplomatic, or military-technical levels. Instead, despite scarce funding, Russia unwisely attempts to carry out a "balanced modernization" of all three legs of its nuclear triad (that is, air-, land-, and sea-based systems), shrinks from discussing tactical nuclear weapons, and seeks to make up for its setbacks through the export of nuclear technologies and materials, as well as massive arms sales abroad.

As early as 1993, democratic Russia officially repudiated the no-first-use commitment made by the totalitarian Soviet Union in 1982. During 2000 and 2001 Moscow reconfirmed that position, and it now says that nuclear weapons play a leading role in ensuring Russian national security. Moscow even acknowledges the possibility of "a selective and limited combat use" of strategic nuclear weapons in order to "de-escalate the aggression."[2] This implies accomplishing specific tasks involved in conducting and terminating nuclear warfare, rather than merely deterring aggression through the capacity to inflict "devastating retaliation," as previously claimed by Soviet official military doctrine.

Not surprisingly, Great Britain, France, and China are not going to undertake any limitations of their nuclear forces through arms control treaties, alleging that they lag far behind the two major nuclear powers. Indeed, all three are implementing planned long-term modernizations and, in some weapon systems, a build-up of nuclear arsenals.

Now, as never before, nuclear deterrence looks like the factor most likely to remain a permanent part of international relations, at least until a more devastating or efficient weapon is invented. Moreover, this posture is taken not because of the colossal technical or political difficulties of achieving "general and complete nuclear disarmament," but because of the presumably considerable "inherent advantages" of nuclear weapons as a means of sustaining national security and "civilizing" international relations by making nations more responsible. Obviously, the Big Five (United States, Russia, Great Britain, France, and China) openly or tacitly treat nuclear deterrence as an indispensable and legitimate instrument of their security and military policies, even as they claim that other countries have no right to acquire nuclear weapons.

Using the traditional Chinese mode of presenting intellectual subject matter (and paying respect to the newly acquired popularity of China's doctrines and policies among some Western and Russian experts), in this study the research is built around a concept that may be called "3 × 3 × 3" (or a "cubed triple") package of paradoxes, assertions, and proposals:

- There are three major paradoxes of post–Cold War nuclear deterrence in the world.
- There are three principal reasons why nuclear deterrence will not serve great powers' national security, and international security, in the long run.
- There are three main avenues of action to transform mutual nuclear deterrence into a more constructive and reliable model of strategic relations while staying short of "general and complete nuclear disarmament."

General and complete nuclear disarmament, as noble a goal as it is, seems at present very distant and unrealistic, because it would require immense changes in the way international politics has been conducted and conflicts have been resolved throughout known history. Such changes are clearly far outside the purview of this book.

As for the "cubed triple," we believe that the decade and a half that has elapsed since the end of the Cold War has demonstrated at least three great paradoxes in regard to nuclear weapons. The first is that mutual nuclear deterrence between the United States and the Soviet Union (and now Russia) has quietly outlived the two states' global rivalry and confrontation, with which it was closely associated from 1945 to 1991, and which continued in its self-perpetuating momentum even after the collapse of one of the main subjects of deterrence—the Soviet superpower. These inexorable dynamics of mutual nuclear deterrence have acquired a growing and negative "feedback effect" on political relations between former opponents, sustaining a muted though multifarious fear: of the supposed evil intentions of the "strategic partner"; of inadvertent or accidental nuclear attack; of possible loss of control over nuclear weapons leading to their acquisition by rebel groups or terrorists; of the one's plans to gain control over the other's nuclear weapons or to deliver a disarming strike against nuclear sites—all this in the absence of any real political basis for suspecting such horrific scenarios or actions.

The second paradox is that with the removal of the fear of escalation of any nuclear weapon use to a global catastrophe, the United States, Russia, and some other nuclear weapon states have become much more casual about contemplating initiation of the actual combat use of nuclear weapons in service to specific military missions. Thus, the end of the Cold War has actually lowered, not raised, the nuclear threshold, to say nothing of bringing an end to nuclear warfare planning altogether.

The third paradox is that with the end of the Cold War, the focus has been on doing away with nuclear arms limitations and reductions, transparency, and confidence building, rather than doing away with nuclear deterrence and eventually the nuclear weapons themselves. The victims of this process (primarily at the initiative of current U.S. policy makers) already include the ABM treaty, START II, and the START III Framework Treaty (an agreement on delineation between strategic and tactical BMD systems), as well as near-term entry into force of the Comprehensive Test Ban Treaty, constructive negotiations on the Fissile Material Cut-off Treaty, and potentially even the Nuclear Non-Proliferation Treaty—at least that is how it looks from the results of a disastrous review conference on that treaty in May 2005. The whole structure of nuclear arms control is collapsing, with most dire predictable consequences from the growth of new threats and risks.

Of the three main reasons why nuclear deterrence should be superseded by some type of constructive strategic relationship between the United States and Russia, and eventually among all nuclear weapon states, the first is nuclear deterrence's irrelevance to the real threats and challenges of the post–Cold War era. Deterrence remains effective against the least probable or nonexistent threats: nuclear or massive conventional attacks by great powers (and their alliances) against each other. But it does not work against new "real and present dangers" such as nuclear proliferation, international terrorism, ethnic and religious conflicts, drug and arms trafficking, transborder crime, and illegal migration. Whether nuclear disarmament might prevent nuclear proliferation is a highly debatable point. It is certain, however, that nuclear deterrence cannot stop proliferation, and it is quite probable that deterrence encourages further expansion of the "nuclear club."

The second reason for replacing deterrence with a new strategic relationship is that the relations involved in mutual nuclear deterrence place tangible limitations on the ability of great powers to cooperate genuinely in dealing with new threats and challenges. The degree of cooperation of the Cold War times, when most arms control treaties, including the Nuclear Non-Proliferation Treaty, were concluded, is not enough for the new era. Such endeavors as cooperation between the two states' secret services and special forces, joint counterproliferation policies (for example, Russian participation in the Proliferation Security Initiative, and envisioned actual U.S.-Russian combat operations against terrorists and rogue and failed states), officially

initiated joint early warning and BMD systems, much stricter
nuclear and missile export control regimes, greater emphasis
on securing and accounting for nuclear warheads and nuclear
materials (which implies broad transparency and access to each
other's secret sites), verifiable cessation of production of weapons-grade nuclear materials throughout the world, and ambi-
tious Global Partnership projects all require a greater magnitude of trust and cooperation among partner states. But all of
these are impossible to imagine while the United States and
Russia still aim thousands of nuclear warheads at each other,
keep missiles on hair-trigger alert, and modernize nuclear forces
to preserve robust retaliatory capabilities against each other.
Besides, as mentioned above, the momentum of nuclear deterrence in combination with new threats and missions may destabilize strategic relations among the great powers, further
undercutting their ability to think and act together.

The current crisis over the Iranian nuclear program, despite
the apparent similarity of the U.S. and Russian positions, provides a good illustration of this point. Neither the United States
nor Russia wants Iran to have uranium enrichment or plutonium reprocessing capabilities, to say nothing of the potential
effect of Teheran's acquisition of nuclear weapons. However,
action in the form of United Nations Security Council sanctions
against Iran, or a UN resolution calling for the use of military
force, is where U.S.-Russian unanimity stops. For the United
States, the prospect of eventually being targeted by Iranian
nuclear missiles is totally unbearable and warrants all means of
prevention. For all conservative Russians, the dire political, economic, and security implications of supporting (even if pas-
sively) UN sanctions or U.S. military action against Iran—
Russia's long-standing partner—may be seen as too high a price
to pay. After all, as hard-liners would point out, Russia is already targeted by thousands of U.S. nuclear weapons, as well
as by the nuclear weapons of American allies and partners (Britain, France, Israel, and Pakistan). A nuclear-armed Iran would
not add much to this picture, and probably would target its
missiles elsewhere anyway.

The prospect of Iranian nuclear materials or weapons being leaked to Islamic terrorist organizations is much more frightening. However, Russian hawks would claim that this is a hypothetical scenario, while actual transactions of that kind might have been already discussed or attempted through A. Q. Khan's black market connections with the Taliban, Al Qaeda, and Iran— without ensuing aggressive U.S. attempts to investigate and prosecute the case. Apparently, this benign position was motivated by Washington's desire not to destabilize its partner regime in Pakistan. As for Russia, its political-strategic elite would be deeply split if it had to make a choice between cooperation with its partner regime in Iran and cooperation with the United States, particularly in view of the state of U.S.-Russian strategic relations.

The third reason for a new strategic relationship is the problem of resource allocation. Sustaining nuclear deterrence at current levels, or even at reduced levels (such as the 1,700 to 2,200 deployed warheads called for under SORT), is an expensive luxury, given that the two biggest powers assign the bulk of these forces the mission of destroying each other, as well as serving "as a hedge against future uncertainty." This aimless "hedge" may be relatively inexpensive for the United States, which has the largest overall defense budget in the world (about as big as the sum of all military spending by the other major powers), and which fully modernized its strategic nuclear force during the 1980s and 1990s, investing in "strategic capital" that will last for decades into the future. Still, even for the United States it would be easy to find a much better allocation of these resources, whether within its defense budget or outside it.

The burden of maintaining robust nuclear deterrence is heavier for Russia, which is now implementing a "balanced modernization" of all elements of its strategic triad and planning to keep up with the SORT ceilings of 1,700 to 2,200 warheads. Faced with having to fund an enormously expensive process of military reform, as well as extensive modernization and restructuring of its conventional forces, Russia nonetheless suffers the expenditure of huge sums on nuclear weapons. The budget share for nuclear deterrence is relatively even bigger for France, Britain, and China.

By maintaining mutual nuclear deterrence, the great powers are wasting resources that otherwise could be applied to more appropriate military and security tasks and missions. Moreover, significant scientific and technical intellectual resources are tied up by nuclear deterrence. Powerful state, business, research, and political organizations are locked into sustaining nuclear confrontation in economic, technical, and mental respects, instead of addressing the more realistic and urgent needs of national and international security.

Another, more general objection to nuclear deterrence is not directly linked to nuclear weapons, so it is not included in our $3 \times 3 \times 3$ package. Still it is worth mentioning. Russia's domestic economic and political evolution is inseparable from its foreign policy. It is impossible to imagine Russia evolving as an advanced market economy and democracy without good relations with the United States and gradual economic, political, and security integration with the European Union.

For the West, consistent cooperation with and integration of Russia is potentially an immense asset in providing for security in Eurasia. The benefits include gaining from Russia's science, technology, and cultural resources; coping with the unpredictable future of the supply of energy and raw materials; containing Islamic radicalism; addressing the proliferation of WMD; dealing with international terrorism; and managing relations with a growing China.

Mutual nuclear deterrence between Russia, on the one hand, and the United States, Britain, and France, on the other, is a latent but real barrier to such cooperation and integration. Although it would be presumptuous to claim that Russian democratic development and economic reform directly depend on doing away with nuclear deterrence, transforming deterrence as part of a process of forging closer security relations with the West would certainly advance Russia's progress toward democracy and economic integration with the West.

The first of the three avenues toward the end of nuclear deterrence is to "de-alert" and further reduce the Russian and American nuclear forces. The second is to develop and deploy a joint ballistic missile early warning system (BMEWS) and a missile proliferation monitoring system. The third is to develop and deploy joint BMD systems. Initially, the second and third avenues would be limited to nuclear and missile proliferation threats, but eventually—in parallel with transformation of the nuclear forces of both sides—they would embrace a growing part of the strategic assets of the two powers and their allies, and would transform their present mutual nuclear deterrence into a qualitatively new type of strategic relationship.

This new relationship could be called "nuclear partnership," "joint management of nuclear weapons," "cooperative nuclear weapons policies," "a common nuclear security framework," "a mutual nuclear insurance [or assurance] strategy," or any number of other names, depending on one's tastes and semantic skills. In any case, the main problem is not the term, but the substance, and it is the substance that is the subject of this book.

Chapter 2 of this book deals with the historical experience of nuclear deterrence. Presently, as applied to the policies of the Big Five, nuclear deterrence is commonly perceived as something that emerged naturally in past decades and that provides a guarantee against a third world war. Historical and methodological analysis does not support such an assessment, although neither does it refute it completely. In contrast to claims made by many politicians and experts, the evolution of nuclear deterrence, along with its character and impact on the likelihood of war, looks more ambiguous. Analysis of this matter gives much food for thought and creates apprehensions concerning the past and future of nuclear deterrence in strategic relations among the Big Five powers.

Chapter 3 addresses the basic aspects of the nuclear policies of Russia and the United States, and outlines the policies of Great Britain, France, and China. The Big Five's strategic concepts, forces, and programs of nuclear force development are investigated, for these factors are much more reliable indicators of an actual nuclear policy than official political declarations, which tend to be ambiguous and controversial.

Chapter 4 addresses the present dynamics of nuclear deterrence, its feedback effect on political relations, and the relevance and potential new roles of arms control in the post–Cold War era.

Chapter 5 describes possible measures for transforming U.S. and Russian offensive nuclear forces, in order to stabilize their balance at still-lower levels (in view of some destabilizing prospects), to move them away from hair-trigger alert status, and to unlock them from overwhelmingly targeting each other. These initial steps would lay the groundwork for abandoning mutual nuclear deterrence as the cornerstone of the strategic postures of both nations.

Chapter 6 presents proposals for building on the initial initiatives to do away with mutual deterrence by integrating the early warning systems and antimissile defense systems of the United States and Russia. Methods of integrating third nuclear weapon states into the new mode of strategic relations are also suggested.

In the conclusion, general observations are offered on the dialectics and dilemmas of nuclear weapons, as well as a detailed list and tentative time frame for technically, strategically, and politically realistic steps to be implemented bilaterally and multilaterally to achieve the stated goal: getting free of the exhausting, deadlocking chains of nuclear deterrence.

Notes

1. An explanation by Sergei Ivanov of the goals and tasks of the Russia nuclear forces; in Russian, 2004, available at www.rol.ru/news/misc/news/04/07/14_010.htm.
2. *Aktualnye zadachi razvitia Vooruzhennykh Sil Rossiyskoi Federatsii* [Urgent tasks of the armed forces of the Russian Federation]. (Moscow, 2003), pp. 41–42.

CHAPTER TWO

The Inherent Contradictions of Nuclear Deterrence

Despite common expectations in the late 1980s and early 1990s, nuclear weapons and concepts for their further development and deployment (which constitute the notion of nuclear deterrence) have survived the end of the Cold War. As the twenty-first century begins, they seem likely to be around forever, even if in new military balances and new international settings.

Even when political relations between certain nations change drastically and they stop viewing each other as enemies, their armed forces face new opponents and new targets presented by nuclear proliferation. This may in many cases destabilize strategic relations between the former enemies and lead once again to an increased emphasis on nuclear confrontation and competition in their strategic relations, with all of the attendant political, security, and treaty-related consequences.

After the end of Cold War, nuclear deterrence (at least between Russia and the United States) began to be seen as only secondarily important. Although they continued to maintain thousands of nuclear warheads, the two former adversaries significantly reduced their nuclear forces and largely curtailed programs to renovate them, at least in comparison to the era of the fast-paced arms races of the 1950s (the bombers race), 1960s (the ballistic missiles race), 1970s (the MIRV race), and 1980s (the counterforce-MIRV and cruise missile races). Although there were serious disagreements over international issues such as NATO expansion and the war in Iraq, confrontation was replaced by growing economic and political cooperation. There was also cooperation in securing and eliminating stocks of nuclear and chemical weapons and nuclear materials, and in dismantling nuclear submarines.

Even as the United States and Russia have reduced their nuclear arsenals and made plans to continue doing so, the nuclear forces of other nations have grown significantly both in absolute and relative terms, and seem likely to keep growing. Figure 2.1 depicts the worst-case scenario. What is more probable in the next ten to fifteen years is "8+2" (the eight states that currently possess nuclear weapons plus North Korea and Iran), or "8+3" (with the additional state being Japan). Worst-case scenarios, however, should not be discarded, and the final outcome may be even more worrisome than that illustrated by figure 2.1. Arab states might eventually overcome their rivalries and join financial, technical, and political resources to create collectively owned and operated nuclear weapons (thus doing something NATO failed to do in the early 1960s). The Pacific Ocean states of Indonesia, Vietnam, and Australia could also join the "club." These developments would have enormous international, political, and military consequences, even in the face of continued overwhelming nuclear superiority on the part of the United States, Russia, and possibly China over any other nation or coalition of nations with nuclear weapons.

Hence, it is not surprising that since the early 1990s, nuclear and missile proliferation, and, later, nuclear terrorism, have moved to the center of international security anxieties and policies of the United States, and (at least at a declaratory level) of other great powers following the U.S. lead.

At the same time, despite growing concerns about proliferation, attitudes toward nuclear disarmament have changed profoundly. Today, nuclear disarmament seems like a romantic relic of the Cold War, when its desirability was almost an article of

Figure 2.1. Worst-Case Scenario, 2015: Changes in the Size of the "Nuclear Club" and the Size of Individual Arsenals

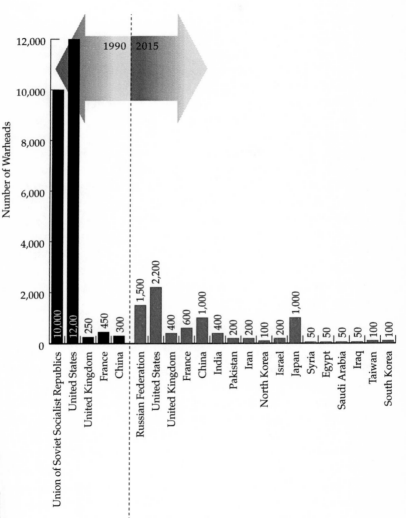

faith, and the great powers were doing everything they could to prove themselves "true believers" and their opponents "sinners" in the eyes of world opinion.

In contrast to the past, the United States, the Russian Federation, and other major powers have in fact abandoned the idea of nuclear disarmament as an intrinsic, if not near-term, condition for finite overall nuclear security. They are disassembling the entire complex of accords on central nuclear disarmament in order to ensure maximum freedom of action for themselves in the technical development and planning of real combat application of nuclear weapons, as reflected in their official military doctrines, armament programs, and budgets.

As never before, nuclear deterrence now appears to be a permanent factor in international politics—at least until even more destructive weapons are invented. This is due not only to the difficulty of achieving complete nuclear disarmament but to the significant advantages that are supposedly inherent to nuclear weapons in providing security and "civilizing" international relations by encouraging restraint in the use of force. A historical analysis of the evolution, present state, and future prospects of nuclear deterrence—along with its various modes and practical implementation in weapon systems and operation plans—raises serious doubts about such a benign evaluation of the doctrine.

The Problems Inherent to Nuclear Deterrence

As long as nuclear weapons exist, nuclear deterrence will remain the most important means for the indirect use of this type of weapon and the basic element of strategic relations with the nations that possess this kind of weapon. In an ideal world, nuclear deterrence would mean that nuclear weapons were not a means for waging war. Rather, they would be political instruments that guaranteed that nuclear weapons would not actually be used in practice—neither in the context of a premeditated attack, nor as a result of the escalation of a non-nuclear conflict between nuclear powers. In the sixth decade of the nuclear era, this view is commonly taken for granted. However, historically, this has not always been so, and the validity of this theory of strategic behavior has always been, and continues to be, subject to question. As for the future, it may be quite different and more controversial still.

Deterrence and Warfare

In order for nuclear weapons to be used as an instrument of psychological pressure intended to deter an enemy, a full military political theory had to be created, which did not happen immediately. Throughout the 1940s and 1950s, atomic and hydrogen warheads deliverable as bombs dropped by aircraft and warheads in missiles were produced by the United States in huge numbers. They were generally considered to be weapons of total destruction of an enemy's armed forces and urban-industrial targets if the Soviet Union were to attack U.S. allies in Europe or Asia. This was the strategy of "massive retaliation."

If deterrence had any place in this strategy, it was as a secondary product or a political byproduct, not the main goal of U.S. military policy and forces development. Only by the end of the 1950s, following fifteen years of nuclear weapon stockpiling and, most important, after the Soviet Union had developed similar weapons and delivery systems, did the concept of deterrence occupy center stage in American military and political strategy. Only then did the political leadership in the United States grudgingly recognize that nuclear weapons are not viable for direct military use. As President Dwight Eisenhower was the first to say at the chief executive level in the mid-1950s, "only a lunatic would see victory in the total destruction of a human race." In the meantime, the number of nuclear bombs reached many thousands, and land-based and sea-based ballistic missiles began to enter service.

Strategic theory in the United States was developed not by generals, as a rule, but by civilian specialists, including natural and social scientists. The works of theoreticians such as Henry Kissinger, Bernard Brodie, Thomas Schelling, Albert Wohlstetter, Adam Yarmolinsky, Wolfgang Panofsky, Robert Bowie, George Kistiakowsky, and George Kennan gave rise to a theory that saw nuclear arms not simply as a more destructive means of waging war but as a qualitatively new kind of weapon that could destroy the entire world and leave no victors. This led to the epochal conclusion that nuclear weapons must be used not for defeating an enemy in war but for preventing such a war from happening in the first place, or, more accurately, for dissuading a potential enemy from undertaking actions that could culminate in a big war.

In the 1960s, following a number of experiments with the concepts of "counterforce" and "damage limitation," U.S. nuclear strategy firmly settled on the concept of "assured destruction." The chief theoretician and practitioner of this strategy was Secretary of Defense Robert McNamara and his civilian assistants, called "whiz kids" (Alain Enthoven, Herbert York, George Rathjens, Jack Ruina, Harold Brown, Daniel Ellsberg, and others). It presupposed maintaining a strategic arsenal capable of surviving an enemy nuclear strike in sufficient numbers to cause the enemy unacceptable damage in a counterstrike (which was set to be an immediate destruction of up to 70 percent of the industrial potential and 25 percent of the population).

No doubt, even under McNamara's rule in the Pentagon, U.S. official doctrinal declarations were not fully reflective of actual operational planning (that is, target lists and the single integrated operational plan). Such planning included first-strike and launch-on-warning options, in addition to second strike, and emphasized attacking military sites rather than urban-industrial targets. Still, official doctrines reflected Washington's general ideas of strategic forces development and deployment and employment criteria, as well as the logic of sufficiency, which was persuasively demonstrated by McNamara's "flat of the curve" models of assured destruction. This philosophy of sufficiency and a less biased view of the main opponent's motives for a nuclear weapons buildup (the so-called action-reaction phenomenon) provided the conceptual framework for the practical strategic arms control and reductions talks and treaties of the 1970s to the 1990s, which contrasted with the propagandistic "talk shows" around "general and complete nuclear disarmament" of the late 1940s to early 1960s.

The Soviet Union arrived at similar conclusions about nuclear weapons, nuclear war, and sufficiency significantly later, since no social scientists, natural scientists, or military officials could freely discuss such topics. All were expected to follow unswervingly the dogmas of Marxism-Leninism and the wretched official military doctrines spun by the military leadership. At the ideological level, the theory of deterrence was branded the handmaiden of the "aggressive policy of imperialism," against which stood the "peace-loving course of the USSR." All of this was against the background of Soviet premier Nikita Khrushchev's hysterical missile bluff, which also was a kind of "offensive deterrence," or, more accurately, an effort to "spook" the West during the Suez, Berlin, and Cuban missile crises of the 1950s through the early 1960s. At the level of military strategy, under the careful watch of the Main Political Directorate of the Soviet Army and Navy and the marshals of the respective armed services (all heroes of the Great Patriotic War), strategists explained nuclear weapons simply as significantly more destructive arms that fit readily into the canon on conducting and winning a world war.

Based on certain connections between politics and military strategy, strategic theory in the West was enhanced by free discussion between political scientists and military experts and greater availability of military information, as well as the regular movement of civilians and military personnel between government posts and the academic world.

By contrast, in the Soviet Union there were watertight separations between politics and strategy and civilian and military specialists, and complete defense secrecy. Hence, the fundamental thesis of Soviet military doctrine was that the Soviet Union's policies were peaceful, but if war began, the army and the people, "under the wise leadership of the CPSU [Communist Party of the Soviet Union]," would achieve the defeat of the enemy and be victorious. The nuclear and conventional armed forces of the country were to be ready for this victory, to which end they were to work to achieve supremacy over the enemy and be ready to undertake offensive action. The thought that these preparations in themselves could cast doubt upon "peaceful" Soviet policy and impel the other side to undertake countermeasures was considered a monstrous heresy. Through the late 1960s, expressing such a thought could cost individuals their freedom, and even through the early 1980s could result in drastic career consequences.

Only at the beginning of the 1970s did the Soviet Union start to change its official position on nuclear war and weapons. With many conditions and reservations, the idea was accepted of the impossibility of gaining victory in a nuclear war because of its massively destructive consequences. Consequently, the view was adopted that nuclear weapons were good only for "deterrence against imperialist aggression." This shift was greatly facilitated by the ideological argument with China (reflecting the great political schism in the communist world), whose leadership was openly pronouncing the possibility of achieving the victory of communism through all-out nuclear war. In 1982, Moscow took a symbolic but politically significant step toward reinforcing the strategy of deterrence by declaring that it would not be the first to use nuclear weapons.

With the demise of the Soviet Union in 1991, the situation in Russia changed fundamentally. Access to military information, open discussion, and professional mobility for military and civilian specialists all increased, as did freedom of thought and expression. But in many respects the Soviet heritage has been kept alive to the present day—there is still inadequate access to information, and decisions on military matters are made completely behind the scenes. Most important, there is a stable stereotype of reasoning that military matters are the affair of the military and political matters are the affair of the politicians and political scientists. To a great extent, this has bred the contradictions and inconsistencies in Russian foreign and military policy in particular and in national security policy generally.

In practice, the relationship between the two principal views on nuclear weapons (as tools of deterrence or as means of waging war) is at once both contradictory and moot. Strategic nuclear forces are carrying out the political mission of deterrence solely through their capability to conduct military operations. They have operational plans, lists of targets, and flight programs entered into the on-board computers of ballistic and cruise missiles. The operational plans, as a rule, anticipate the use of these weapons at some level of effectiveness for the planned first strike, preemptive strike, delayed retaliatory strike, launch on warning, and launch under attack. The latter two scenarios require launching upon receiving signals from satellites in space and the ground-based radars before the enemy's warheads reach their targets or as they are exploding over their targets.

In theory, the needs of pure deterrence (the absence of fighting) could be met simply with realistic replicas of missiles and aircraft, while the exclusive task of fighting a war (the absence of deterrence) could be performed by nuclear arms whose existence was kept in full secrecy. In reality, though, with the systems that actually exist—land-based ICBMs, submarine-launched ballistic missiles, and heavy bombers armed with gravity bombs or air-launched cruise missiles—the line between deterrence and warfare has always been vague. Hence, it is more appropriate to think instead in terms of the priorities of various kinds of operational plans or target lists, which in turn reflect priorities given either to deterrence or to actual warfare.

For example, weapons that have high survivability and are targeted on industrial sites (submarine-launched ballistic missiles of lesser accuracy and land-based mobile ICBMs) may be considered objectively more suitable for a retaliatory strike, and thus serve as primary weapons of deterrence policy. Conversely, weapons that are more vulnerable at their launch positions or that are targeted mainly on the enemy's nuclear and conventional forces (ICBMs with multiple warheads launched from fixed silos and submarine-launched ballistic missiles with accurate high-yield warheads) objectively indicate priorities of a strategy for actually conducting war. In this case, nuclear weapons are primarily assigned to deliver a disarming (counterforce) or damage-limiting strike, which may be interpreted as having the goal of winning a nuclear war. The logic here is that it is precisely the certainty of terrible losses that makes victory unattainable and nuclear war itself unthinkable; hence a strategy of avoiding or limiting damage may indicate the goal of winning nuclear war or making it more acceptable. Theoretically, it is possible to deter the enemy by a strategy of winning nuclear war, but since it is predicated on one's own first nuclear strike, it cannot logically be seen as deterrence of nuclear attack by the opponent.

In the Soviet Union in the late 1970s and early 1980s, the strategic nuclear force corresponded more closely to the model of forces for war fighting (about 70 percent of warheads were on silo-based ICBMs with MIRVs), although at the political level deterrence was placed at the forefront. As it has since the 1990s, and likely will continue to do through the near future, the strategic nuclear force will correspond predominantly to the deterrence (second-strike) model. First-strike (counterforce) capability will degrade, as will survivability if the present modernization program is not corrected or new arms control agreements are not achieved. Paradoxically, at the declaratory level since 1993 the openly proclaimed mission of Russian nuclear weapons is to be available for first-strike use and selective strikes, which is associated much more with warfare than deterrence.[1]

It is interesting to note that in the 1950s and 1960s Soviet forces also corresponded objectively to the deterrence model in their capabilities, though out of a lack of any ability to deliver a disabling strike against the United States. In light of dogmatic ideology and the complete closure of military policy to outside criticism, however, their doctrinal goals were to "defeat the enemy decisively" and to "win in global nuclear war." At the same time, first use of Soviet nuclear forces could be motivated by their high vulnerability at launch positions and the ineffectiveness of Soviet command, control, communication and intelligence system and early warning systems, which left little hope that these forces could survive a preemptive U.S. nuclear attack, at least until the mid-1960s when a sufficient number of ballistic missile nuclear submarines and silo-based ICBMs were deployed. (At that time and until the late 1970s, hardened silos provided high levels of survivability against ballistic missiles, given their relatively poor accuracy. The much higher accuracy and yield of MIRV warheads has made silos vulnerable since the early 1980s.)

The United States' nuclear weapons were openly intended for victory over the Soviet Union and China through the total destruction of their military potential and administrative and industrial centers. In the 1950s this doctrine was based on the fact that the continental United States was out of range of the Soviet Union's nuclear weapons. After losing this geographic advantage during the first half of the 1960s, U.S. war-fighting strategy relied on the fact that the American strategic nuclear force was many times larger than its Soviet counterpart (which was seen as a basis for counterforce or damage-limitation strikes), and on the existence of forward-based nuclear forces in Eurasia capable of enhancing a disarming strike on the strategic forces of the Soviet Union. Only after the mid-1960s, with the growing size and survivability of the Soviet strategic nuclear force, and in particular as a result of the political experience of the 1962 Cuban missile crisis (which revealed the dubious practical applicability of nuclear war-fighting plans), did the concepts of "conducting war" and "deterring war" switch places in Washington's military policy, seriously and for the long term, in favor of deterrence.

In the 1970s and 1980s, and especially the 1990s, despite the increasing accuracy, selectivity, and flexibility of each country's strategic nuclear force, the fact that the strategic balance between the United States and the Soviet Union (and, later, Russia) had evened out and retaliatory capabilities had become more assured worked to increase the emphasis on deterrence. Negotiations on the Strategic Arms Limitation Treaty (SALT) and START were progressing and political relations were improving, which also helped. Subsequently, in the 1990s even deterrence was deemphasized in the two powers' political relations, which became focused more on cooperation and partnership.

In the near future, the relationship between deterring and conducting war in Russian military policy may become even more ambivalent. With the maintenance of generally good political relations between the Russian Federation and the United States, both the doctrine of mutual deterrence and the military and technical reality standing behind such deterrence would be of very little importance. But if political tensions rise, the leadership in Russia might be faced with a very unpleasant reality.

Decisions made in Russia in 2000 and 2001 to transfer resources to the conventional forces from the strategic nuclear force brought little tangible benefit to the former while deeply hampering the latter. As a result, in ten to fifteen years more than 90 percent of the Russian strategic nuclear force could be exceedingly vulnerable to a salvo of less than a hundred Trident-2 submarine-launched ballistic missiles, which corresponds to the capacity of just three or four (of fourteen) U.S. strategic submarines. By contrast, 80 percent of U.S. nuclear forces (in numbers of warheads) will be secure against attack, and the United States simultaneously will have a high disarming counterforce strike capability against the Russian strategic nuclear force. These conditions all fall within the limits of SORT, the U.S.-Russian treaty of 2002 calling for the reduction of strategic offensive weapons to 1,700 to 2,200 nuclear warheads.

In contrast with its U.S. counterpart, Russia's strategic nuclear force and command, control, and intelligence system would not be able to survive a first strike by the United States and inflict a more or less equal amount of damage in retaliation. The only way the Russian force could cause such damage would be by carrying out a preemptive strike or launch-on-warning strike in response. In the case of a preemptive strike, Russia would subsequently suffer total destruction through nuclear retaliation by the United States and its allies. The poor condition of the Russian Missile Attack Early Warning System would make a launch-on-warning strike an almost equally futile option. The warning system has become unreliable as a result of degradation of its space systems and the fact that more than half of its radar stations lie outside Russian territory. Technical breakdowns in warning systems or errors in the evaluation of information when there is absolutely no time to spare in deciding whether to launch missiles would create a harrowingly high risk of an inadvertent first strike, with, again, the annihilation of Russia the likely result. This risk will only grow as the world enters a state of multipolar nuclear balance and an expanding number of nations have ballistic missiles with nuclear warheads positioned near Russian territory (see figure 2.2).

It is possible not to worry about these apocalyptic scenarios because of the nearly unthinkable nature of a deliberate nuclear war between Russia and the United States. However, if one accepts that deterrence indeed plays a role in preventing war and ensuring security, and that it will remain as a basis of the U.S.-Russian strategic relationship for a long time, then the technical and military state of deterrence is also of serious significance. Otherwise, one would have to conclude that mutual deterrence is simply irrelevant to security in U.S.-Russian strategic relations, despite relatively large resources dedicated to its maintenance (especially by Russia) and the absence of any alternative mode of nuclear postures and strategic relations between the two nations. Operating under the latter conclusion would be quite a schizophrenic way of thinking about nuclear weapons. Historically, such a mentality may not be unprecedented, but it clearly should not be desirable in the post–Cold War era of partnership and cooperation.

As for the present moment, factors of single order must not be viewed in different planes. The decision by the Russian leadership to extend the service life of the heavy SS-18 ICBM and purchase SS-19 ICBMs from Ukraine, as noted by President Putin at the General Staff conference on October 2, 2003, in order to maintain the numerical levels of the strategic nuclear force and its capability to defeat "any BMD system," was intended exclusively to deter the United States (albeit with obsolete systems that were already vulnerable to a hypothetical strike by U.S. Peacekeeper and Trident-2 missiles as far back as the late 1980s). It is too early to speculate on the cost-effectiveness of the new strategic system with gliding and maneuvering warheads, whose development was announced by the Russian president in early 2004, but it is clear that this system would also be assigned the mission of deterring the United States through countering its BMD deployment program. Likewise, the development of an expensive new system of nuclear submarines with ballistic missile launch capability, for deployment in northern

Figure 2.2. Potential Threats to Russia from the Proliferation of Regional WMDs and Missile Technology

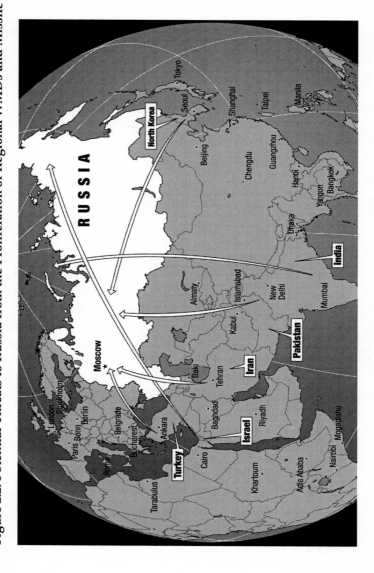

waters, has no other evident purpose than to bolster deterrence against the United States and NATO.

The United States takes the task of maintaining robust deterrence no less seriously in strategic and technical terms, even though this stance is no longer overtly declared in official nuclear posture and policy statements. The U.S. deterrence posture has multiple operational options and a huge "margin of safety," and remains overwhelmingly oriented toward Russia. For example, the United States' reluctance to reduce its strategic nuclear force to less than 1,700 to 2,200 warheads, its insistence on maintaining a two-ocean Trident-equipped ballistic missile nuclear submarine navy (to cover thoroughly the European part of Russia as well as China and Russian Siberia), its relocation of counterforce W-87 warheads from dismantled MX Peacekeeper missiles to Minuteman-3 ICBMs, its retention of several hundred tactical nuclear bombs in Europe, and other choices are all indicative of such a strategic policy.

Since maintenance of a deterrent capability is considered so important by both sides, the fact must not be taken too lightly that the Russian strategic nuclear force planned for the next ten to fifteen years will have a steadily declining capability of surviving a first strike, except by launch on warning. Moreover, continued reliance on the concept of launch-on-warning will pose a greater danger of a nuclear war by accident, miscalculation, or third-party provocation.

The present situation illustrates the first problem inherent to nuclear deterrence: It is meaningless without the capability of strategic forces to conduct actual combat operations. At the same time, preserving such a capability may oblige Russia in the near future to rely increasingly on first-strike or launch-on-warning concepts that are prone to a catastrophic collapse of deterrence leading to inadvertent nuclear war. In an acute crisis, a Russian first strike or launch-on-warning strategic posture might make it appear that a nuclear exchange was unavoidable, and thus could provoke the United States to capitalize on its huge nuclear superiority by initiating a preemptive strike. Knowing this, Russia, in turn, might become still more trigger happy. Under such conditions, political miscalculation, technical failure, a provocative third-party's missile attack, or a terrorist nuclear explosion in either (or both) capitals might trigger a nuclear holocaust, a disaster that the two nations managed to avoid during the four decades of the Cold War.

Thus, deterrence between Russia and the United States may contain the seeds of its own collapse. This prospect is not only supported by the miscalculations of Moscow's current strategic modernization program but by Washington's disinclination to continue nuclear arms reduction and limitation talks, to say nothing of jointly elaborating a new policy designed to supercede mutual nuclear deterrence with an alternative kind of strategic relationship, immune to traditional factors of instability.

Tactical Nuclear Weapons

Even more than with the strategic weapons, the "gray zone" of ambiguity between deterrence and nuclear warfare affects operational-tactical and tactical nuclear weapons, sometimes also called substrategic nuclear arms. This is the second problem inherent to nuclear deterrence.

Tactical nuclear weapons traditionally have been deployed mainly on dual-use delivery systems: strike aircraft; mid-range bombers; artillery and surface-to-surface rockets for ground forces; demolition munitions (for example, nuclear mines); antiaircraft air-to-surface missiles and air defense fighter-interceptors; naval rockets and torpedoes of various types on submarines and surface ships; and carrier-based and land-based naval aircraft. At the peak of the Cold War, the United States had up to 20,000 tactical nuclear weapons, and the Soviet Union had more than 30,000 tactical nuclear weapon warheads. Even now, based on available information, the United States and Russia continue to maintain thousands of nuclear weapons of this class, while 200 to 400 U.S. tactical nuclear bombs remain stored in Western Europe.

Although in the broadest sense the presence of tactical nuclear weapons in the conventional Western and Soviet/Russian forces may be said to make up part of nuclear deterrence, in practice these weapons have always been seen primarily as arms for fighting a war, at least much more so than the strategic weapons. In light of their destructive power, tactical nuclear weapons were viewed as helping to achieve a quicker success in the theater of military operations or to compensate for enemy superiority in conventional forces. Such views affected the policies for producing, perfecting, storing, deploying, and using tactical nuclear weapons, as well as the principles for authorizing their employment and guarding against their unauthorized use, which are much less stringent than those for strategic nuclear forces.

Regarding tactical nuclear weapons, it is nearly impossible to draw a line between deterring and waging war. At the same time, however, the very differentiation of nuclear weapons into strategic and tactical categories is itself very contextual. For the Soviet Union, the American tactical nuclear weapons, in the form of the forward-based nuclear systems in Eurasia, were always equated with strategic weapons, since they could reach deep into Soviet territory if fired from forward bases or from surrounding seas. For Western Europe and the Soviet Union's neighbors in Asia, the Soviet tactical nuclear weapons were equivalent to strategic weapons in terms of range and destructive power.

Because tactical nuclear weapons are much more closely intermingled with conventional forces both technically and operationally than strategic nuclear forces, they can be quickly integrated into conventional warfare, either as munitions on dual-purpose delivery systems or as targets of conventional strikes (whether intentional or not).

As long as tactical nuclear weapons remain an element of the U.S. and Russian nuclear arsenals and operational plans, the line between nuclear deterrence and war, or between nuclear first and second strikes, or even between conventional and nuclear war, will remain blurred. This will add another element of instability to the U.S.-Russian nuclear deterrence relationship.

"Enhanced" and "Extended" Deterrence

The third general problem inherent to nuclear deterrence lies in the ambiguity that exists at the very core of the concept. In common usage, deterrence implies that nuclear weapons will deter a potential opponent from implementing a nuclear strike. This function is called "minimal" or "finite deterrence," and logically implies the ability and probability of a second strike by a small and relatively invulnerable force on a limited number of the aggressor's most valuable administrative and industrial targets.

The forces and the concepts of "minimal deterrence," in whatever terms it has been formulated by the two states at the official level, in fact were maintained by the Soviet Union against the United States until the mid-1960s. They were maintained by Great Britain, France, and Israel against the Soviet Union until the end of the 1980s (after which the nuclear firepower of Great Britain and France grew sharply with deployment of MIRVed missiles), as well as by China against the Soviet Union until the early 1990s and, most likely, against the United States in the near future.

Nuclear weapons were, however, frequently intended not only to deter enemy nuclear attack but to deter other undesirable actions, foremost being aggressive use of other types of WMD or conventional forces only, as well as other actions that could lead to an armed conflict. This application is called "enhanced deterrence." This version of deterrence is much more widely used than is usually assumed, while what is thought of as deterrence in general is only one of its types—"minimal deterrence." In thinking about broader notions of deterrence, it is not always understood that these notions usually imply the first use of nuclear weapons—that is, the initiation of a nuclear war.

Naturally, each side contemplating nuclear first use to deter conventional aggression assumes that it would be acting in a purely defensive and legitimate way, and that all the responsibility for nuclear war would lie with the aggressor. But in reality, the aggressor and the victim are not always clearly defined and broadly agreed upon in an armed conflict. Examples from the Cold War are the wars of the 1950s through the 1980s in Korea, Indochina, and Afghanistan; the three wars in the Middle East; and, following the Cold War, the wars in Yugoslavia in 1999 and Iraq in 2003. Characteristically, in none of these instances did those on either side of the conflict recognize themselves as aggressors. Neither the United Nations nor the international community was unanimous on this point either. Theoretically, both sides in any of these conflicts, if it were facing defeat and possessed nuclear weapons, could have considered themselves justified in using those weapons first to achieve enhanced deterrence.

Since the end of World War II, the United States relied on enhanced deterrence to prevent an attack by the superior conventional forces of the Soviet Union and Warsaw Pact against its allies in NATO, and in Asia to prevent an attack by the Soviet Union, China, or North Korea on U.S. allies in the Western Pacific. Washington has never abandoned this kind of deterrence and has always implied its willingness to use nuclear weapons first in extraordinary circumstances. In recent times, Washington has made clear that this doctrine would be applied to "rogue nations" in the event that they used chemical or bacteriological weapons against the United States, or were understood to possess nuclear capability. This was recently the main justification for plans to develop new types of nuclear warheads capable of destroying command bunkers and WMD storage facilities.

Soviet and now Russian military doctrine has also long included a nuclear first-strike policy. This was rescinded in 1982, but openly revived in 1993, and confirmed in a clarified form in 2000. Enhanced deterrence for Moscow's part unambiguously assumes a first use of nuclear weapons "in response to large-scale aggression by conventional weapons in situations deemed critical to the national security of the [Russian Federation]."[2] It is clear that Russia now views deterrence specifically in its enhanced version, in light of the growing inferiority of its conventional forces to those of NATO, and Russian forces' impending wide inferiority to those of China. Enhanced deterrence might be theoretically justified by the disparity in conventional forces, but it could work in practice only if it were reinforced not just by a declared willingness to use nuclear weapons first but by the corresponding material balance of nuclear forces. Put simply, it requires superiority over the other side both in tactical and strategic nuclear forces, so that an enemy would not have the potential at either level to preemptively disarm Russia, or to inflict on it unacceptable damage in retaliation.

For that reason, the Russian strategy is hardly credible with respect to NATO. After all, with a growing quantitative and qualitative supremacy in conventional forces, NATO could rapidly create superiority in tactical nuclear weapons by bringing U.S. weapons into the theater. Meanwhile, the United States (especially when considered in combination with Great Britain and France) will for the next ten to fifteen years continue to expand its strategic nuclear superiority over Russia, including the capability to deliver a disarming strike against Russian tactical and strategic nuclear forces.

It is true that Russian deterrence of the West may not cause concern, since deliberate conventional or nuclear war between Russia and the European Union or the NATO states is unthinkable. The economic and political interests of the democratic countries of Western Europe, and the unacceptability to their populations of even minor losses, serve as the primary guarantee against attacks on the Russian Federation or its allies. But if, hypothetically, in place of the Western European powers there were an aggressive authoritarian power (or union) with the same military capabilities, then the Russian strategy of enhanced deterrence in its current mode would be put to a severe test.

Consequently, the strategic situation along Russia's eastern borders cannot but cause concern. At present, both the political relations between Russia and China and the balance of military forces between them are satisfactory from the standpoint of security. But in ten to fifteen years relations could worsen, and there might be grounds for a conflict of interest between the two countries, while the balance of forces, both conventional and nuclear, including the strategic forces, could significantly shift to the detriment of the Russian Federation, and thus signal the demise of enhanced deterrence as applied to Sino-Russian relations.

Within Russia, the present deterrence strategy is commonly supported simply because there is no systematic open discussion of such matters in the country. There is also no broadly knowledgeable parliament, mass media, or public organizations to serve as a forum. The military and political leadership feels that it can ignore independent criticism from individual experts and make all decisions behind the scenes.

Other nations have also endorsed the strategy of enhanced deterrence, for example, Great Britain and France, in declaring that their nuclear forces existed not only to deter a nuclear strike by the Soviet Union but also an attack by conventional Warsaw Pact forces. But unlike NATO in regard to Russia, neither Britain nor France had the nuclear potential to provide the objective basis for enhanced deterrence of the Soviet Union. They did have, however, a strong protector and defender in the United States, whose huge nuclear umbrella provided extra protection while these two countries tried various strategic experiments. In the coming ten to fifteen years, the nuclear forces of Great Britain and France (with full complements of warheads for their MIRVed submarine-launched ballistic missiles) will become comparable to the Russian strategic nuclear force for the first time in history, while the number of warheads on highly survivable missiles capable of mounting counterforce strikes will for the first time exceed the Russian total, even without counting U.S. systems.

Israel has employed a variation of enhanced deterrence by using weapons from its unacknowledged nuclear arsenal to deter attacks by the conventional armies of Arab nations. If a critical situation arises, Israel will make a first nuclear strike against them. Israel's strategy explains its attack on the nuclear reactor in Iraq in 1982 and its alarm at Iranian nuclear programs. This strategy was quite credible as long as the Arab countries and Islamic states outside the Arab world did not have their own nuclear weapons, a situation that changed in 1998 with Pakistan's evident development of an atomic military device. The impact on Israel's nuclear strategy remains unclear.

The objective geostrategic difference between the United States and the Soviet Union and its Russian successor has shaped both countries' use of enhanced deterrence. Because the United States' geographic location and its sea power has made a large-scale conventional attack on it virtually impossible, the option of first use of nuclear weapons in response to conventional aggression is only associated with defense of U.S. allies in Europe and East Asia. Hence, for the United States a more apt term to define its strategic doctrine would be "extended deterrence." This model anticipates the granting of a nuclear guarantee for the security of allied nations: that is, a promise to use nuclear weapons in response to an attack on U.S. allies by either the conventional or the nuclear forces of a common enemy.

For the Soviet Union, and still more for Russia, the geostrategic situation has been different in that Moscow not only has had to uphold its commitments to its allies but has had to take into account the contingency of being directly attacked by the conventional forces of its enemy in either the west or the east. True, for the Soviet Union this arrangement was not too daunting in view of the conventional superiority it and its Warsaw Pact allies enjoyed over NATO and China. For Russia, which is becoming ever more inferior in conventional forces, and which has also lost most of its allies while facing NATO and Chinese forces right on its borders, the concept of enhanced deterrence occupies the central place in doctrine and strategy beside the concept of extended deterrence.

For half a century, extended deterrence was the basis of allied relations in NATO and the Warsaw Pact. It continues by default to the present day in NATO, even though the nations of Western Europe are no longer threatened by any attack from the east. Moreover, NATO has a growing supremacy over Russia in conventional forces and in the near future will gain supremacy in nuclear weapons as well.

It is clear that the concept of extended deterrence provides for the first use of nuclear weapons and thus the initiation of nuclear war. But in contrast to the situation under the strategy of enhanced deterrence, these actions (subject to the most catastrophic consequences, especially if the enemy also has nuclear weapons) must be undertaken not for the sake of protecting the vitally important interests of one's own country, but for the sake of another nation.

To have credibility, an extended deterrence strategy must rely either on a nuclear weapons monopoly or overwhelming nuclear superiority over the opponent. In 1949, the United States gave guarantees to NATO that were based on its nuclear monopoly. But in 1952 Great Britain developed its own atomic device, in order to avoid full reliance on the willingness of the United States to keep its promises in case of a major war in Europe. After the Soviet Union developed ICBMs, France also began to doubt the reliability of U.S. nuclear guarantees, which added to its determination to acquire its own nuclear weapons (which it did in 1960), and in 1967 France left the NATO military organization. Thus did the French express mistrust about U.S. promises, in the vernacular of the day, "to trade New York for Paris" in case war broke out. As strategic parity developed between the Soviet Union and the United States, American extended deterrence under NATO became even more dubious, causing deepening conflicts within the alliance (i.e., the crises of the early 1980s, precipitated by U.S. deployment of medium-range missiles in Europe). But then the Cold War ended unexpectedly, the Warsaw Pact and the Soviet Union collapsed, and the question of the reliability of American nuclear commitments was removed from the NATO agenda.

Russia readily made similar promises about nuclear protection to its allies in the Commonwealth of Independent States and in the CIS Collective Security Treaty of 1992. Perhaps Moscow was so willing because a direct attack on Russian allies from abroad is not considered very likely. It might also be that extended deterrence is not given too serious a meaning, or that the underlying strategic sense of such guarantees is simply not understood by the present Russian political leadership and military commanders. In any case, while Russia's allies under the Collective Security Treaty are not threatened by aggression from a nuclear power (or union), the guarantees of extended deterrence have a certain, if mostly empty, appeal. But if the situation were to change in the future, the Russian leadership might face an agonizing decision on whether to support the credibility of its promise to "trade Moscow for Minsk or Yerevan" (not to mention Dushanbe, Bishkek, or Astana).

Thus, yet another factor of great ambiguity in nuclear deterrence in the modern world is the fact that, in contrast to how it is widely presented, in only a few cases and for limited periods has deterrence been perceived and practiced in the narrow meaning of the concept—that is, as a strategy for preventing nuclear war. Much more frequently, deterrence is given a broader strategic meaning that provides for the first use of nuclear weapons. This is yet another inherent contradiction in nuclear deterrence: It commonly assumes the willingness to initiate a nuclear war. Fortunately, over the past half-century this apocalyptic paradox has remained mostly in the domain of theory. But in the future, the proliferation of nuclear weapons and the increasing multipolarity of nuclear relationships among states threaten to place it in the range of the practical.

The Ostensible Rationality of Nuclear Deterrence

The idea of nuclear deterrence has so engrained itself into military and political relations among nations over the past half-century that it is universally accepted as completely rational and lacking in alternatives. Without a doubt, nuclear deterrence is less irrational than the doctrine of actually conducting nuclear war, especially between nuclear powers. However, if judged from other than a strictly military and strategic perspective, for example, the social and political point of view, then the rationality of deterrence looks much more dubious.

Even the more defensive (in the sense of excluding first strike) and stabilizing variant of this strategy—"minimal deterrence"—is paradoxical. After all, what is being suggested is striking back to retaliate for a nuclear attack by destroying tens of millions of civilians in the other country. This act of revenge, in the first place, would be irrational, since the slaughter of the population of the other country would not return the lives of the citizens of the attacked country nor regenerate its destroyed resources. More than that, in contrast with the strategic conventional bombing of Germany and Japan in World War II, as controversial as they were, a nuclear strike against civilians would in no way affect the ability of the enemy to continue the war, which would depend entirely on its surviving nuclear weapons and the functioning of its command-and-control system.

In the second place, if in the prenuclear age it was impossible to start or conduct a war without the support of at least a portion of the population in the aggressor's country, a nuclear war can now be started without any agreement on the part of the nation, simply through an order from its leaders to the crews of the missile launch control centers (and in the newest command-and-control systems, bypassing even them and connecting directly with the launchers). The people, who are the main targets in a nuclear exchange, would have no direct responsibility for the aggressive decision made by their government. This would be especially true in authoritarian and totalitarian regimes, where the people not only do not elect their own leaders but may not even be seen by the latter as being of the greatest value. This attitude toward the population was demonstrated, for example, by the leadership of the People's Republic of China when, in the 1950s and 1960s, it proclaimed total war as the path to "final victory" over imperialism.

At the end of the 1970s, suspecting the Soviet leadership of the same attitude toward its people, President Jimmy Carter issued Presidential Directive 59, in which he advanced a "countervailing strategy" calling for strikes against what the Soviet leaders were thought to value above all else—their own lives. This meant the destruction of the hardened underground bunkers and bomb shelters, as well as other sites where Communist Party and government leaders could take refuge. It goes without saying that this concept evoked an extremely painful reaction in Moscow, where it was called the "strategy of decapitating strikes" and evaluated as the latest scandalously aggressive step in the American strategy of launching a disarming strike against the Soviet Union. This fear led to enhanced Soviet reliance on a launch-on-warning strategy, which thus increased the danger to both sides.

Other attempts to make nuclear deterrence more rational also, as a rule, had the opposite effect. For example, the improved ability of strategic nuclear forces to launch counterforce strikes against the aggressor's reserve strategic forces, which may not have been used during its first strike, would definitely be seen as an enhancement of the potential for making not a second strike but a disarming first strike. This perception was not without justification: The missile launch silos, submarine and bomber bases, and deployment areas of the land-based mobile ICBMs are the very targets that need to be taken out in the first strike in order to avoid retaliation or to reduce damage from it. The response to such strategic experiments, aside from increasing the survivability of strategic nuclear forces, has generally been to give greater priority to the concept and technical systems for launch-on-warning strategies and to plan for the use of greater numbers of weapons.

Hence, the principal attribute of nuclear deterrence is that while being generally accepted by politicians and the public in peacetime, it could suddenly look horrible in a crisis situation, when it is really supposed to do the job of preventing war. It is then that its practical implications come to the forefront of decision makers' deliberations. Since deterrence may fail in many ways (crisis escalation, technical accident, miscalculation by the military, etc.), the decision to execute the threat on which deterrence is based seems to be the ultimate irrationality. As a rule, efforts to enhance the credibility of deterrence by improving its applicability (for example, through selective targeting and reduction of the collateral damage effects of the nuclear weapons, or through plans for the use of limited numbers of warheads) are usually perceived by the other side as indicating movement toward an increasingly aggressive nuclear strategy that includes a first-strike capability for the purpose of winning a nuclear war.

The fundamental paradox of nuclear deterrence lies in the fact that the deterrence posture, which makes nuclear war the most unthinkable (massive strikes, maximum damage, high speed and certainty of retribution—up to a fully automatic nuclear counterattack, called "doomsday machine" in the U.S. and "dead hand" in the Soviet Union) would be the worst option if deterrence failed and nuclear weapons were actually used, since it would lead to a total mutual annihilation of the opponents. But at the same time, attempts to make the use of nuclear weapons more rational in case deterrence fails tend unavoidably to lower the "nuclear threshold" and weaken deterrence itself, by making nuclear war less unthinkable.

Perhaps the most important factor in the paradoxical nature of deterrence is that, given the catastrophic consequences of using a nuclear weapon, especially using it in error, no other class of arms needs to be controlled by the political leadership to such a great extent. The paradox is that at the same time it is more difficult to ensure real political control over the use of nuclear weapons than of any other kind of weapon. This is because of the technical characteristics of nuclear weapons, in particular strategic nuclear forces, which would require the actions of thousands of people at all levels, operating the most technically complex systems, to be synchronized to the minute. This synchronization would have to occur under intense pressure and in a situation in which the systems of command and control, early warning systems, and the weapons themselves were all being targeted by the enemy's nuclear forces and might be hit at any moment. All of the following would have to be considered: the flight time of strategic missiles (maximum of 30 minutes for ICBMs, minimum of around 10 minutes for submarine-launched ballistic missiles); the time needed to receive, verify, and evaluate the signals of early warning systems; the time needed to issue the order for subordinates to launch missiles; and the time to prepare the launch, fire a missile from its silo, and have it get away from the probable attack zone. In the best-case scenario, the top leadership would have only several minutes to make a political decision. In the worst-case scenario, the leadership would have "negative time"—that is, the flight time of the enemy's missiles would be less than the time it would take to receive and evaluate the attack information, plus the time needed to launch a missile counterstrike of one's own (see figures 2.3 and 2.4).

Moreover, at such times the leadership will act on the basis of reports from subordinates and their evaluations of the situation, and will not be able to recheck this information or depart from established operational plans. Otherwise, leadership would have to face the risk that a retaliatory strike would not be implemented at all. In essence, the role of leader is relegated to a formality. This loss of executive control is particularly evident in the context of the concepts of launch on warning and launch

Figure 2.3. Timeline for Command-and-Control and Missile Attack Warning System Functions (ICBM Attack Scenario)

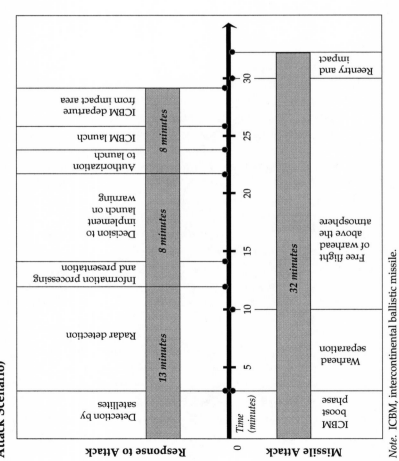

Note. ICBM, intercontinental ballistic missile.

Figure 2.4. Timeline for Command-and-Control and Missile Attack Warning System Functions (SLBM Attack Scenario)

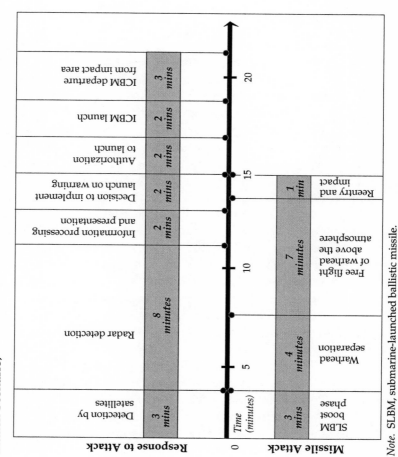

Note. SLBM, submarine-launched ballistic missile.

under attack, and will be greatly aggravated by the growth of the number of countries possessing nuclear missiles and with the broadening of the scope of potential attack azimuths.

During peacetime, state leaders, to judge from the numerous pronouncements they make on the subject, never get around to thoroughly studying the apparently surrealistic scenarios of, and plans for, nuclear war. Heads of state seldom have access to independent critical expertise that could disabuse them of many of the absurd and dangerous notions that underlie nuclear military planning (and those with such expertise usually do not possess top-secret information on the subject). Yet in the course of routine operational planning, the military is always making the guarantee of launching nuclear weapons under the worst circumstances (called "positive control") its top priority, instead of guarding against the inadvertent outbreak of nuclear war, unauthorized actions, false signals, or technical breakdown ("negative control"). Numerous organizational and technical trade-offs between positive and negative control are usually resolved in favor of the former, because implementing the assigned mission is always the military's top priority.

In a real crisis, if the use of nuclear weapons is no longer an abstraction but a reality, there will be neither the option nor the time to review the technical characteristics of various systems or the operational plans for using nuclear weapons. Thus, the government leadership will be held hostage to secret departmental decisions that were closed to any criticism and adopted many years ago in different circumstances and based on completely inappropriate considerations.

An impressive classic historic analogy, with all the conditionality that accompanies such analogies, is provided by the plans for troop transport by rail made by the German General Staff before 1914, which, naturally, Kaiser Wilhelm II and his government were loath to review during peacetime. In the summer of 1914, with the onset of the international crisis that preceded World War I, the German leadership found itself faced with a choice: Either begin the planned shipments under the well-known Schlieffen Plan, which provided for an attack to the west and then to the east, or change the plan and doom the troop movement to chaos and Germany to a two-front defeat in the upcoming war. Berlin chose to adhere to the original plan, prepared through the scrupulous technical work of military specialists during peacetime, based on strictly operational considerations and blind to all dramatic turns and dilemmas of the political crisis of 1914. The political leadership ended up hostage to a preplanned military strategy and the military technical base of operational planning. This made World War I unavoidable—with the well-known consequences for Germany and the entire world, felt all the way to the end of the twentieth century.

A profoundly influential historical analysis of the development of that tragedy was presented by the American historian Barbara Tuchman in *The Guns of August*.[3] President John F. Kennedy read this book shortly before the Cuban missile crisis of October 1962, and was deeply impressed by it. At the time of the missile crisis, he and the leader of the Soviet Union, Premier Nikita Khrushchev, had nearly crossed the Rubicon of nuclear conflict, both men being trapped in the dynamics of military and political escalation and barely in control of the situation, with incomparably worse potential consequences than those of August 1914. It could be that Tuchman's book prompted Kennedy to exercise extra caution, maintain flexibility, and adopt a more critical attitude toward the recommendations from the U.S. military command in those dramatic days.

Unfortunately, from all appearances neither Khrushchev nor his Soviet and Russian successors have read books such as *The Guns of August*. Neither is it clear whether subsequent American leaders have read such books. Otherwise, they would have scrutinized the details of U.S. nuclear strategy and weapons programs much more deeply during peacetime, bringing in independent experts and refraining from relying totally on the military agencies, so as to retain real control over the course of events when the fateful hour comes.

Mutual Deterrence—The Rule or the Exception?

Analysis of historical experience and the present situation shows that the relations of mutual deterrence between nuclear powers are more of an exception than a rule, especially if stable deterrence is meant, which is supposed to minimize the probability of nuclear war. Aside from all of the above-mentioned specific versions of deterrence, mutual deterrence may be understood at the most general level to exist in two forms.

One form of mutual deterrence may be called "existential deterrence"—the political and psychological effects of prudence and caution that nuclear weapons are able to inspire in the opposing side(s) by the mere fact of their presence. This is independent of technical characteristics, numbers of such weapons, or these weapons' command-and-control systems and effectiveness. "Existential" deterrence is inherent to nuclear weapons simply in light of a certain probability of their use in the event of war, inasmuch as one or more sides in the conflict do possess them, and because of the huge destructive consequences of the use of even individual weapons of this kind. At the same time, the role of such a level of deterrence is heavily dependent on factors such as the acuteness of conflict in the political relations of the sides, the degree to which third countries would get involved, and regional military balances. If the crisis is severe indeed, and there are no allied obligations on the part of third powers, existential deterrence could lead to the outbreak of a nuclear war, since the state that launched a first strike would in most cases gain great military advantage.

In contrast, the other general form of mutual deterrence, which may be called "qualified deterrence," assumes the reasonable likelihood that the nuclear forces will succeed in meeting whatever specific goals they have been given under the assumed circumstances of the outbreak of war. There are numerous versions of qualified deterrence, ranging from "minimal" to "extended." A variety of versions of qualified deterrence have been seen in various countries at different times. Qualified deterrence, understandably, is a much more reliable and predictable means of ensuring the defensive capabilities of a nation, in that it is assumed to provide for a reasonable level of strategic stability despite any tension in international relations and even during times of crisis between states. Also, it may create the material basis for nuclear weapons limitation and reduction agreements as valuable specific tools for ensuring mutual security, transparency, and greater trust between nations.

The classic version of qualified deterrence, which is mutual and decreases the probability of nuclear war in particular and armed conflict in general to a minimum, is the strategic relationship between the United States and the Soviet Union (and now Russia) from the late 1960s to about 2010 or 2012. After this, Russian deterrence will predictably become minimal, then perhaps even existential, at least with respect to strategic relations with the United States (see, this chapter, "Deterrence and Warfare"). That is, of course, if the Russian Federation's nuclear forces development program is not corrected in the near future to provide for much higher second-strike capability than presently projected and no new arms control agreements are reached.

Until the mid-1960s, the British and French nuclear forces in themselves could muster only existential deterrence against the Soviet Union, while from the mid-1980s to the mid-1990s they were capable of minimal qualified deterrence. During this whole time, the Soviet and, later, Russian strategic nuclear force had the overwhelming capability to launch a disarming strike against Britain and France. Only the alliance with the United States and its nuclear guarantees under NATO allowed the British and French to experiment freely with their nuclear forces and concepts, using them for the goals of prestige and as factors in relations with allies, with no real fear for their own security. For the next ten to fifteen years, while the Russian strategic nuclear force is shrinking and the potential of British and French weapons is increasing, Britain and France will attain parity with Russia in the capacity for qualified deterrence.

After developing nuclear weapons in the mid-1960s, China had the potential for only existential deterrence against the Soviet Union, and no reliable deterrence at all against the United States until the early 1970s. By the 1990s, China had acquired the capability for a minimal deterrence against Russia and existential deterrence against the United States. Based on the rates of production and modernization of the Chinese strategic nuclear force, over the next ten to fifteen years China might acquire the capability for a robust qualified deterrence against Russia (together with superiority in conventional forces in East Asia) and minimal and qualified deterrence against the United States.

Having obtained a nuclear capability at the beginning of the 1980s, Israel had by the end of the decade gained the capability for qualified deterrence against its region's Arab states, which lacked such weapons, and existential deterrence against the Soviet Union.

Over the next few years, India and Pakistan will have the classic version of mutual existential deterrence, which is exceedingly unstable and dangerous with respect to the outbreak of nuclear war in a serious regional conflict. At present, both states evidently lack efficient command-and-control systems (in particular, negative control systems to prevent an unauthorized missile launch), and keep their missiles separate from their nuclear warheads. Such a regime is better than if both India and Pakistan had fully coupled nuclear forces: Both states' missiles are vulnerable to a disarming strike, both nations lack early warning or reconnaissance systems, missile flight times are extremely short (five to ten minutes), and official military doctrine allows for a first nuclear strike (equivocally for India and unequivocally for Pakistan).

Since entering the "nuclear club," the two states have shown greater political caution in crises and have agreed on notification of missile launches and some confidence-building measures. Their mutual nuclear deterrence, however, remains extremely fragile since neither party has the monitoring capability to confirm whether the other's missiles and warheads are decoupled. If some future crisis escalates to an armed conflict, both nations would rush to couple missiles and warheads, after which there would be a strong incentive for India to implement a preventive conventional or nuclear-conventional counterforce strike, while for Pakistan there would be an irresistible motive for preemption on the basis of the "use-it-or-lose-it" theory.

In the early missile era, both the United States and the Soviet Union (much like India and Pakistan today) kept their first-generation ICBMs decoupled from warheads, but after a few years, with technical improvements, they abandoned this practice and deployed permanently armed missiles. India and Pakistan will probably follow this trend. In that case, there may be a more stable deterrence on the peninsula if both nations, beside coupling their missiles and warheads, simultaneously acquire more effective command-and-control systems (including permissive action links such as an ability to technically ensure both positive and negative control over launch) and reconnaissance capabilities (air- or space-based), as well as survivable missile-basing modes (hardened silos and ground-mobile or sea-based forces). Otherwise, their nuclear balance will become highly unstable. Taking this into consideration, the United States and Russia might render technical assistance in some of these areas in exchange for the two nations' entry into bilateral arms control talks and various nuclear arms control regimes.

A still-better alternative would be for India and Pakistan to reach an agreement to keep missiles and warheads separate, and to agree on reliable verification provisions for this agreement. For this, U.S.-Russian sponsorship might be an effective tool as well. India and Pakistan could even serve as a test model of one of the methods of implementing a possible future U.S.-Russian de-alerting and deactivation regime.

Besides the India-Pakistan nuclear balance, India will in the near future have existential deterrence with respect to China, which will maintain its significant nuclear supremacy over India until it gains qualified deterrence in five to ten years. If it has not already, Pakistan will soon gain existential deterrence against Russia (technically covering a large part of its Siberian territory), despite Russia's clear nuclear superiority.

If North Korea and Iran are allowed to create their own nuclear weapons in the near future, the maximum they would be able to gain is existential deterrence against the United States. This prospect might become the strongest factor provoking a use of force by the American side, possibly including a preemptive air and missile attack with high-precision conventional weapons and even nuclear strikes. The chances of a U.S. strike could increase depending on whether the United States can deploy a genuinely effective antiballistic missile system on U.S. soil.

On the whole, it must be concluded that, despite the perceptions broadly accepted after the end of the Cold War on the stabilizing role of nuclear weapons, relations based on a qualified mutual deterrence are a rare phenomenon indeed. From Figure 2.5, it is clear that relations between countries possessing nuclear weapons may not be based on deterrence in a number of situations:

- when the nuclear weapons of the two sides are deployed out of range of each other's territories or important foreign targets: Britain and France, on the one side, and China, India, and Pakistan on the other
- when targets may be within range of each state's weapons, but the states are all military and political allies: the United States, Britain, France
- when two states are within each other's range and do not have formal alliance relations, yet still do not have nuclear deterrence relations because the nuclear weapons of each side are obviously directed at a third power: India and Russia, Pakistan and China, Israel and France
- when one power has significant superiority in offensive or defensive weapons, in which case deterrence might be predominantly unilateral and unstable: the United States and China, North Korea, or Iran, as well as, potentially, the United States and Russia
- when two states' nuclear weapons are vulnerable and there is a lack of reliable command-and-control and early warning systems, in which case deterrence may be fragile and mutually dangerous: India and Pakistan, Israel and Iran, North Korea and Japan, South Korea, or Taiwan (provided that Iran and North Korea and its three potential adversaries "go nuclear").

From this analysis it follows that a stable mutual nuclear deterrence relationship is and has been the exception rather than the rule. Hence, there is no reason to hope that in the future nuclear relationships between and among new nuclear weapon states, and even between some traditional nuclear powers,

Figure 2.5. Bilateral Deterrence Relationships Matrix

	United States	Russia	Great Britain	France	China	Israel	India	Pakistan	North Korea	Iran
United States		O			⊙				⊙	⊙
Russia	O		O	O	O	⊙		⊙		
Great Britain		O								⊙
France		O								⊙
China	⊙	O					⊙			
Israel										⊙
India					⊙			⊙		
Pakistan		⊙				⊙	⊙			⊙
North Korea	⊙									
Iran	⊙		⊙	⊙		⊙		⊙		

O = stable
⊙ = unstable

would remain a solid guarantee against actual nuclear war, as it has for the past sixty years. Moreover, even when past experiences are considered, it is not an absolute truth to assert that deterrence has had a role in preventing nuclear war.

What Prevented a Nuclear War?

Was nuclear deterrence a real factor in preventing total war in past years? Considering the rigid bipolarity and acute confrontation that characterized international relations from the late 1940s to the early 1970s (two conditions that historically have always preceded great wars), it is possible that if the major opposing sides, otherwise evenly matched, had not had nuclear weapons, a third world war would have in fact happened. According to this line of reasoning, it is possible that the existence of nuclear weapons exerted a constant and unseen influence, playing the role of an inherent deterrent factor independent of the military and technical specifics of the ever-changing nuclear balance between the opposing sides.

At the same time, it must be remembered that the nuclear arms race in and of itself became an important factor in tensions between the opposing sides and that it gave rise to periodic crises in relations—for example, the crisis arising from the deployment of U.S. medium-range missiles in Europe in 1983. What exactly prevailed in the sense of greater or lesser probability of war will forever remain a topic of speculation.

The only example of a direct effect of mutual deterrence would be in a situation in which the nuclear and conventional forces were placed on high alert in anticipation of war, but the powers then stepped back from the brink out of fear of nuclear catastrophe. This kind of classical episode happened only once— in October 1962, during the Cuban missile crisis. It is true that at that time the deterrence emanating from the Soviet Union was more existential than qualified, since the Soviets had only several operational ICBMs, which were completely vulnerable on open launch pads. The U.S. leadership knew this but could not be absolutely certain, given the level of effectiveness of the reconnaissance systems of that time. Besides, the Soviet Union had a number of long-range bombers and many medium-range missiles and bombers, which could devastate U.S. allies and forward-based forces. Hence, some kind of mutual nuclear deterrence did exist, though in an asymmetric form.

Only one factor prevents this instance from being firm confirmation of the positive role of nuclear deterrence. This is the fact that the crisis of 1962 was predominantly caused by the very dynamics of nuclear deterrence. Moscow decided to deploy medium-range missiles in Cuba in order to close the growing gap with the American strategic nuclear force and forward-based nuclear forces. And the sharp acceleration in U.S. ICBM and submarine-launched ballistic missile programs was implemented in response to a bluff by the Soviet leadership regarding their ability to "crank missiles out like sausages."

So it turns out that nuclear deterrence presents yet another paradox: It worked best for preventing a war whose risk was generated by the evolution of nuclear deterrence itself (that is, the cure saves the patient from the illness caused by the cure itself).

Nuclear Deterrence and Terrorism

Nuclear deterrence cannot be used against transnational terrorist organizations, even when such organizations have acquired a nuclear weapon or other explosive device. Terrorists have no territories, industries, populations, or regular armies that can be targeted for retaliation. In instances when they are given a base by a government, such as the Taliban gave to Al Qaeda in Afghanistan, nuclear deterrence with respect to such a state would still find little application, since it would hardly be likely to exert a restraining influence on the terrorists, who have great freedom of movement, including the ability to pass through borders quickly and secretly. It is possible that terrorists would even be interested in provoking a nuclear strike on one of their host countries for the sake of advancing their cause.

The struggle against catastrophic terrorism is related to deterrence only in the sense of deterring (through the threat of retribution, including nuclear reprisal) some countries from supporting terrorism by granting bases or providing other assistance. But it is difficult to imagine that any state would openly support terrorists possessing nuclear weapons. And a nuclear strike on any country, even a "rogue state," considering the secondary consequences and political shock in the rest of the world, would be too blunt an instrument to use without a fully evident corpus delicti. Quite revealing in this regard has been the reaction of the world community to the poorly justified U.S.-led operation in Iraq in 2003, in which only conventional forces were used, and with minimal secondary losses and material damage. The breakup of the antiterrorist coalition to a huge extent has inspired the resistance movement and international terrorism in Iraq and has drawn the United States into the swamp of an open-ended occupation.

This past experience relates directly to the recent American concept of developing "clean" nuclear minicharges that could penetrate deep underground to destroy bunkers, warehouses, and other subterranean terrorist or "rogue state" targets. Even without mentioning the political consequences of such a use of nuclear weapons, from a tactical and technical standpoint the use of nuclear minicharges elicits a great deal of doubt. In order to avoid nuclear contamination of the locale, a subkiloton charge must penetrate the earth to a depth of 150 to 200 meters, which is impossible. Penetration to a depth of 10 to 15 meters is the imaginable technical limit, especially in hard rock formations. Then, the "coupling effect" (of warhead with the surrounding matter) would provide about ten times as great a shock wave effect as an air or surface burst of the same yield. However, at such a depth the collateral damage of a nuclear explosion would be almost the same as that resulting from a surface burst—but with all the ensuing physical, military, and political consequences.

Moreover, if a target is to be destroyed with a penetrating nuclear minicharge, its exact location must be known within a range of no more than a few hundred meters. If the location were already known, however, then contemporary non-nuclear high-precision warheads and high-yield charges could destroy the target, especially if multiple use were an option. Repeated attacks would be possible since such underground sites are not "urgent" targets, which must be destroyed quickly and at once, like ICBM silos. If the target were an ICBM silo or underground tunnel for missile or aircraft, it could be easily destroyed by existing counterforce hard-target killing nuclear warheads. Command bunkers or WMD storage places would not be urgent targets and could be repeatedly attacked by conventional munitions. Also, conventional troops and special forces could be used, particularly if such an operation were conducted by coalition forces and on a legal basis (i.e., under United Nations mandate).

As for the political aspects of the concept of using nuclear weapons for counterproliferation purposes against rogue states or terrorists, a showcase was provided in the spring and summer of 2005, when the North Korean leadership, having violated the Nuclear Non-Proliferation Treaty, withdrew from the treaty and then declared that North Korea had successfully manufactured a nuclear weapon. North Korea was suspected of preparing a nuclear underground test in a well-known location. It would be hard to imagine a clearer and more provocative instance for the United States to demonstrate its will to carry out its counterproliferation strategy. The United States could have attacked and destroyed the nuclear test site and other key nuclear facilities of this classic "rogue state," thereby thwarting North Korea's nuclear weapon development program for many years, possibly forever.

However, instead of using military power, Washington used diplomacy to get North Korea back to a six-party negotiating table. As "ideal" as the setting for the application of military power was, it turned out to be too risky and politically counterproductive to use even conventional precision-guided weapons, which would have a high probability of taking out the dangerous facilities with little collateral damage. It is appropriate to assume that it would be still less thinkable to use a nuclear weapon, even one designed to reduce fallout, against a "rogue state" in a situation other than that of imminent threat of a nuclear attack against the United States. And in such a situation, a great variety of existing strategic nuclear force and tactical nuclear weapon systems would be available.

It is not surprising in this regard that the new American nuclear weapons program was received so poorly in Russia, despite its modest financing and early stage of development. The rumors that periodically circulate that Washington is considering scenarios for a "preventative surgical strike" against Russian nuclear weapons (in the event that Moscow loses control over them) were combined with news of the minicharge program. Thus, it was logical to make conclusions about the minicharges' possible use to disarm the Russian Federation with minimal secondary damage in order not to elicit a retaliatory strike against the United States with the surviving Russian missiles.

Although the earth-penetrating warhead program appears to be blocked at the moment, due to congressional opposition that led to the Bush administration's decision not to request further funding for its development, it may well reappear in one of the administration's future budgets.

For the most part, the struggle with nuclear terrorism consists of active special operations, destruction of material and financial infrastructures, protection of nuclear warheads and materials storage facilities, and, above all, a tightening of the nuclear nonproliferation regime. The key role here is played by cooperation between the great powers and regional participating countries in antiterrorist actions and measures to strengthen the Nuclear Non-Proliferation Treaty regimes, to which U.S. application of a nuclear threat, not to mention the actual use of nuclear weapons, would be a true disservice.

Perhaps nuclear weapons have been a factor in preventing a third world war, or perhaps the human race has just been lucky. If it is just a matter of luck, then it is very good that history has no subjunctive mood. But the evolution of nuclear deterrence in the post–Cold War period, against the backdrop of an expanded geography for local, domestic, regional, and transnational conflicts, in conjunction with the proliferation of WMD and means for their delivery, remains a matter of great uncertainty, and surely too consequential to continue entrusting to luck.

The new, so-called pragmatic approach taken by the United States and, subsequently, Russia and probably other nuclear powers, evaluates the advantages of nuclear deterrence, the political and military applicability of nuclear weapons, and the processes of nuclear weapons limitation and reduction, and, as a consequence, dismantles certain regimes. It is often justified by the changing international security environment. However, such an approach is a faulty response to new challenges; even worse, it creates threats to international security in and of itself.

Thus, another paradox of nuclear deterrence is that it may remain relatively effective against threats that are no longer relevant (aggression by the United States, NATO, Russia, or China against each other) though unable to deter the threats of the present and future. One threat in particular is transnational terrorism, which flourishes in the environment of local conflicts in so-called rogue and failed states. Transnational terrorist groups potentially could be armed with WMD.

The dialectics of nuclear deterrence and proliferation are in agreement with Hegel's classic law: Within every thesis lies its contradiction. In the beginning, nuclear deterrence (as a policy of the indirect use of nuclear weapons for political aims) gave rise to proliferation because more and more countries strove to take advantage of the fruits of deterrence to achieve their interests. As the circle of countries possessing nuclear weapons grew, however, deterrence became ever more ambiguous, unstable, and contradictory. This was explained as being a result of both its expanding multilateral nature and the paradoxes inherent in deterrence, including its ambiguity with respect to the possibility of a first use of nuclear weapons, the dubious rationality of a number of its fundamental assumptions, and the ephemeral nature of the control over its use by the political leadership.

The final stage of proliferation is when nonstate actors (for example, terrorist organizations) gain access to nuclear weapons, which will completely and finally end deterrence as a doctrine of the indirect use of such arms to protect national security. Terrorists need nuclear weapons not for deterrence but for direct use and blackmail of various countries, or of the entire civilized world. In turn, nuclear deterrence on the part of governments is helpless against terrorists.

The dialectics of nuclear deterrence and proliferation have been reflected in the processes of arms reductions and disarmament as well. Born out of the fear of nuclear war, the desire of the leading powers to stabilize mutual deterrence created a basis for agreements on limiting and, later, reducing the number of nuclear weapons. At an early stage in this process (after the Partial Test Ban Treaty of 1963), the end of nuclear proliferation began to be viewed as a mandatory condition for progress toward nuclear disarmament. After the Nuclear Non-Proliferation Treaty was signed in 1968, the powers moved well along the path of partial nuclear disarmament, which would include agreements such as the ABM treaty, SALT I and SALT II, the Intermediate-Range Missile/Shorter Range Missile (IRM/SRM) Treaty, START I, II, and Framework Agreement on START III, the Comprehensive Test Ban Treaty, and permanent extension of the Nuclear Non-Proliferation Treaty.

Arms control did not stop proliferation, though it possibly slowed its progress. It was, however, of great importance for ending the Cold War and the massive nuclear arms race between the United States and Russia. At the end of the 1990s, proliferation accelerated for reasons unrelated to nuclear disarmament. This made proliferation the central concern of the great powers, foremost the United States and the Russian Federation, which was absolutely justifiable. What was not justifiable was abandoning further efforts by these states to reduce and limit their nuclear weapons. A consistent course of further U.S.-Russian nuclear arms control would greatly enhance nonproliferation and provide for a profound revision of an outdated Cold War type relationship of mutual nuclear deterrence.

To defend against states that have recently acquired nuclear weapons (or are suspected of the intention to acquire such weapons), and to fight the threat of nuclear terrorism, the United States, with other powers following its lead, has initiated the development and perfection of defense systems, as well as the creation of a new generation of nuclear weapons to be used preemptively against terrorist bases and the "rogue nations" that give them refuge. With mutual nuclear deterrence the continuing basis of great power strategic relations (thanks in part to the Russian nuclear inferiority complex and its obverse, the United States' nuclear superiority complex), this commitment to defense systems is undermining the foundations of stable mutual deterrence between the main powers. It is also leading to the disintegration of the arms limitation and disarmament infrastructure.

In closing the Hegelian circuit of nuclear dialectics, the collapse of two generations of arms control treaties will most likely destroy the Nuclear Non-Proliferation Treaty and undercut the basis of the main nonproliferation regimes and mechanisms.

Notes

1. *Aktualnye zadachi razvitia Vooruzhennykh Sil Rossiyskoi Federatsii* [Urgent tasks of the armed forces of the Russian Federation]. (Moscow, 2003), pp. 41–42.
2. "Voyennaya doctrina Rossiyskoy Federatsii" ["Military doctrine of the Russian Federation"]. *Nezavisimaya gazeta*, April 22, 2000, p. 74.
3. Barbara W. Tuchman, *The Guns of August* (New York: Macmillan, 1962).

CHAPTER THREE

Nuclear Programs
of the Big Five

In regard to nuclear arms, the real, rather than the declared, policy of Russia, like that of any nuclear state, depends on the actual condition of its nuclear weapons and the armed forces in general, the approved programs for nuclear weapons development, and the existing plans for combat use of the nuclear forces. Of these factors, the plans for combat use are classified, as are, for the most part, the development programs of Russia's nuclear forces.

None of the five states possessing nuclear weapons (the so-called nuclear club, also referred to informally as "the Big Five") makes their plans for combat use public. The exception is the occasional excerpt, never acknowledged officially, from the U.S. single integrated operational plan. The United States, Great Britain, and France release information on their programs of nuclear force development, while Russia and China normally do not, although the Russian special and popular news media often provide factual data and analysis that have the effect of bringing

---

This chapter borrows in part from a research paper, also by the authors, *Nuclear Deterrence and Non-proliferation* (Moscow: Carnegie Moscow Center, 2005).

Russia up to the corresponding Western standards for disclosure. As for plans for combat use and targeting of the Russian nuclear forces, the Russian news media give no information whatsoever, even in the noncommittal form of private experts' conclusions. No official data are available about tactical (that is, operational tactical) nuclear weapons, programs for such weapons' development, or plans for their use. This is why this chapter mainly deals with nuclear forces in the strategic context, with the tactical component covered only in passing.

Nuclear Policy of the Russian Federation

Adding Distance between Russia and "No First Use"

The last official full presentation of the Russian nuclear policy was given in the Military Doctrine of the Russian Federation endorsed by President Putin on April 21, 2000. It is noted in this document that Russia maintains its status as a nuclear power, and proceeds from the need for a nuclear deterrent with a potential for "assuring a preset damage on the aggressor in any conditions."[1]

Following lengthy internal discussion of the doctrine, the Russian government announced that "the Russian Federation reserves the right to use nuclear weapons in response to the use against the country and/or its allies of nuclear or any other types of weapons of mass destruction, as well as in response to a large-scale aggression involving the use of conventional weapons in the situations that are critical to the national security of the Russian Federation."[2] This statement was consistent with a previous document, the Basic Provisions of the Military Doctrine (1993), though in contrast with the no-first-use commitment declared by the Soviet Union in 1982.

The position articulated in 2000 brought the nuclear posture of Russia closer to the principles of nuclear strategy shared for many years by the United States, Great Britain, and France. These countries have never repudiated their Cold War stance of reserving the right to initiate first use of their nuclear weapons if attacked by superior Soviet-led general-purpose forces of the

Warsaw Pact. That is why, given the considerable weakening of the general-purpose forces of Russia, its present doctrine on the use of nuclear forces should be acknowledged as meeting the generally accepted standards, regardless of these standards' reasonableness or conformance to the state of relations between Russia and the West.

The latest version of Russia's national nuclear strategy introduces more novelties. In particular, it assigns a mission of "deescalation of aggression . . . through a threat of launching or actual launching of strikes of a varying scale by using conventional and/or nuclear weapons." Also noteworthy is the policy of "dosed" (selective, limited) combat use of some components of the Strategic Nuclear Forces, as well as the stated intent to demonstrate willingness to use these forces by "enhancing the level of their combat readiness, conduct of exercises, and relocation of some components."[3]

Thus, for the first time, Russia has officially declared that it can conduct a limited nuclear war involving the use of strategic nuclear forces. Further, it has enumerated the measures used to enhance these forces' readiness, such as deployment of nuclear-powered ballistic missile submarines, dispersion of mobile ICBMs, and the movement of heavy bombers to alternate airfields. These steps appear to copy U.S. strategic innovations of the 1970s and 1980s, although through the near future Russia will be using weapons that are expected to be less fit in terms of both number and quality.

Although it is possible that the language on nuclear doctrine is addressed to China, Pakistan, and potential nuclear powers that could challenge Russia, what is clear is that Moscow has finally confirmed that its national nuclear policy is aimed at maintaining approximate parity with the United States in strategic nuclear forces. There is, however, no consensus on the issue within Russia. Some hold the view that the Russian strategic nuclear force should be maintained at a level comparable to that of Great Britain and France. In terms of classic deterrence, this would most likely be sufficient for the post–Cold War period, and if Russia were in the position of developing its strategic nuclear force from scratch, such a position would be quite reasonable. But since actual parity presently exists between the Russian and U.S. nuclear forces and the existing agreements can contribute to maintenance of this parity at a considerably lower level, which is acceptable to the Russian polity in terms of resources, there is no reason for Russia to reject it unilaterally.

Changes in the Treaty System, Changes in Nuclear Priorities

The past few years have seen significant changes in the development program of Russia's nuclear forces as a result of changes in the system of treaty-related strategic relations with the United States, as well as some arbitrary top-level decisions lacking a well-substantiated political, operational-strategic, or military-economic rationale.

The previous program of strategic nuclear force modernization was developed in 1998 by a commission of experts headed by N. N. Laverov, vice president of the Russian Academy of Sciences, with START II provisions in view. It was approved by President Boris Yeltsin. In line with certain financial restrictions, the program called for maintaining a total of 1,500 warheads, including more than 400 single-warhead fixed and ground-mobile ICBMs, with adherence to these levels to begin in 2007. By then, the parties had already signed the draft START III framework agreement of 1997 and had had initial consultations on the modernization issue. It was supposed by Moscow that the treaty would at least remove limitations on development, testing, and deployment of mobile ICBMs with MIRV warheads, since their performance characteristics did not differ in terms of strategic stability from those of the submarine-launched ballistic missiles for which prohibition on MIRVs had never been considered before. If this supposition turned out to be true, it would be logical to maintain the structure of the strategic nuclear force that had existed since the Soviet era, in which the ground-based component accounted for 60 to 70 percent of the warheads.

Subsequently, in 2000 the head of the General Staff of the Russian Armed Forces persuaded the national leadership to revise the approved program for strategic nuclear force modernization and redistribute the funds for modernization in favor of the general-purpose forces. This led to a sharp cut in the land-based ICBM force and seriously slowed the rate of procurement and deployment of new Topol-M (SS-27) ICBMs. In particular, it was proposed by the General Staff that by 2003 the number of warheads on ICBMs be reduced to about 150.[4]

This shift in priorities was and remains a grave strategic blunder for a number of reasons. On the one hand, savings from reducing the ground component of the strategic nuclear force were insignificant compared to the funds directed to development of the general-purpose forces. On the other hand, such a decision remained geared to the expectation of the entry into force of START II, an expectation that was in conflict with the real political situation. It is widely believed in Russia that this arbitrary and unilateral truncation of the ground component, the most effective leg of the Russian strategic nuclear force, made it much easier for the United States ultimately to make the decision to abandon the ABM treaty, START II, and the START III framework.

The Strategic Offensive Reduction Treaty (SORT), signed in Moscow in 2002, specified future limits on Russia's warheads with no other conditions. In a sense the terms are quite acceptable, since replacing START II with the new agreement has removed a number of treaty-related limitations on the maintenance and development of the strategic nuclear force. First, it allows the Russian Federation to prolong for some time the service life of heavy ICBMs that otherwise would have to be discarded by 2007 under START II. Second, Russia can now equip Topol-M missiles with MIRVs. In this case, Russia can easily maintain the strategic force up to the limit of 2,200 warheads, unless it dismantles, ahead of schedule, their basing infrastructure or stops the previously authorized program of producing Topol-M missiles. Fitting the Topol-M with MIRVs would not only effect a relative increase in the total number of warheads in the strategic nuclear force but would also cut the cost of producing the missiles themselves, because far fewer missiles would be needed for the same number of warheads than if the missiles were fitted with single warheads.

The operational status of Russia's strategic nuclear force is classified, at least to the extent possible under the transparency provisions of START I. According to official data in the START memorandum of understanding, in 2005 the Russian strategic nuclear triad numbered 815 delivery vehicles and 3,479 warheads. In particular, there were 545 ICBMs and 1,955 warheads in the Strategic Missile Forces. Sea-based forces consisted of 12 nuclear submarines carrying 192 launchers and 672 warheads. In the air component there were 78 heavy bombers carrying 852 air-launched cruise missiles.

As a result of wrong decisions made during 2000–2001, the long-term strategic nuclear force program does not include a key indicator of strategic stability and robustness of nuclear deterrence—survivability of the nuclear forces, including the command-and-control system, in hypothetical nuclear and non-nuclear wars. In late 2004 and early 2005, various representatives of the Defense Ministry reported from time to time that over the long term the Strategic Missile Forces were planning to acquire a few divisions of mobile Topol-M missiles. However, unless the authorities announce revision of the initial decision to drastically slow down the program, one can assume that the Russian strategic nuclear force will have to rely more heavily on silo-based ICBMs and either the first-strike or launch-on-warning concept. With SS-25 Topol ICBMs being withdrawn as they reach the end of their service life, with heavy bombers losing combat capability and becoming increasingly vulnerable because of concentrated basing, with most of presently operational ballistic missile nuclear submarines expected to go out of service by 2015 and very few new ones being commissioned (and still fewer at sea at any given time), it may take no more than 200 to 300 nuclear warheads (the capacity of just two or three Trident submarines) to destroy 90 percent or more of the Russian strategic nuclear force. Moreover, for the first time in history, the Russian strategic nuclear force may become vulnerable to the nuclear weapons of countries other than the United States.

At the same time, just by maintaining its forces at START I or even SORT levels, the United States will inadvertently gain an overwhelming capability for a disarming counterforce attack against the Russian Federation. This growing instability of the Russian-American strategic balance, occurring against the background of a continuing relationship of mutual nuclear deterrence, would not only be dangerous in a possible crisis, but would hamper deeper cooperation between the two powers in the field of international security, especially where joint military actions (for example, counterproliferation) or joint military-technological programs (for instance, joint missile launch warning systems or BMD systems) are involved.

On the issue of the limitation and reduction of nuclear weapons, Russia presently holds a more traditional position than the United States, especially that of the Bush administration. After ratifying START II in 2000, Moscow advocated the conclusion of a START III and an agreement on delineation of strategic and tactical antimissile defenses. It also opposed the United States' withdrawal from the ABM treaty or proposals for its revision. It also advocated much deeper strategic nuclear reductions under SORT (to 1,500 or even 1,000 warheads) without treating the operationally deployed weapons and warheads in storage as separate categories. Russia ratified the Comprehensive Test Ban Treaty in 2000 and supports its soonest possible entry into force.

Nuclear Policy of the United States

From Planning for Threats to Anticipating "Possibilities"

The nuclear policy of the United States is outlined in the Nuclear Posture Review and the National Strategy to Combat Weapons of Mass Destruction.

The quadrennial review of the new nuclear doctrine sent to the U.S. Congress at the end of 2001 shifted the emphasis in strategic forces planning from the threat-based approaches of the Cold War to new principles. The new nuclear policy appears to differ from that enunciated in Presidential Directive 60, signed by President Bill Clinton in November 1997. Presidential Directive 60 focused on deterring the use of nuclear

weapons and ruled out a Reagan administration recommenda-
tion that the U.S. armed forces should be ready to wage a pro-
longed nuclear war and win it. The 2001 policy also reiterated
the provision set forth in the 1994 Nuclear Posture Review that
the basic targets of the United States' nuclear weapons are the
opponents' nuclear arms and associated infrastructure, rather
than cities and industrial centers.

One of the conceptual premises of the new nuclear policy is
that the Cold War approach to deterrence is no longer appropriate, above all in relations with Russia, which formerly were
built around mutual deterrence through a threat of assured destruction. This provision might be interpreted as refuting the
claim that the Pentagon has no strategic plans for using nuclear
weapons against Russia, China, and several other states. Russian defense minister Sergei Ivanov's comment on the point was,
however, skeptical: "As a head of the military agency I am well
aware that the Ministry of Defense should foresee any scenario,
including the worst cases. No planning is a surprise for me."[5]

The new version of the national nuclear posture elaborates
for the first time a concept of the follow-up stage in the military
foundation of the United States' national security—a transition
to a new triad. Unlike the old triad, which involved ICBMs, submarine-launched ballistic missiles, and heavy bombers, the new
triad comprises an offensive component, including non-nuclear
strategic options; active and passive defense components, including antiballistic missile defense; and a developed defense
industry infrastructure with up-to-date command-and-control
assets, to which the old-type nuclear triad is linked. Apparently,
the new concept formulates a long-term objective—to reduce
the United States' dependence on nuclear weapons and enhance
the capability to contain new threats in an environment of pro-
liferating WMD. At the same time, since a threat of escalation is
no longer treated as critical, as it was in the Cold War era, the
new strategy boldly wipes out the borderline between the use
of nuclear weapons and that of conventional weapons against
potential adversaries.

Thus, it is postulated by the U.S. authorities that offensive
nuclear forces alone cannot deter aggression in the twenty-first

century, as demonstrated by the events of September 11, 2001. At the same time, active and passive defenses are also far from perfect. But while they continue to possess the capacity to prevent limited attacks or at least blunt their effectiveness, these defenses will be able to develop some new capabilities for active operations in settling critical situations, containing threats, and conducting military operations.

The established parameters of the strategic nuclear component for the period beginning in 2020 confirm the continuity of U.S. nuclear policy in terms of the structure and composition of the old triad. As of 2005, the United States had 1,225 delivery vehicles and 5,960 warheads in its strategic nuclear force. In the land-based leg there were 550 ICBMs and 1,700 warheads (500 Minuteman-3 and 50 Peacekeeper MX missiles). In U.S. sea-based forces there were 18 submarines with 432 missiles and 3,168 warheads (including 144 Trident-1 and 288 Trident-2 submarine-launched ballistic missiles). The air leg consisted of 81 B-1, 20 B-2, and 142 B-52 bombers—altogether, 243 airplanes and 1,098 warheads.

Apparently, the forces planned for 2012 consist of 14 ballistic missile nuclear submarines carrying Trident-2 type submarine-launched ballistic missiles; 500 Minuteman-3 ICBMs; 76 B-52H bombers; and 20 B-2 heavy bombers. Minuteman-3 upgrade programs are currently under way, which means that these missiles will be in use at least until 2020. Also, the U.S. Navy has decided to extend the service life of ballistic missile nuclear submarines carrying Trident-2 missiles for another 42 to 44 years. Modernization of submarine-launched ballistic missiles is also planned so that their service lives match those of ballistic missile nuclear submarines. The timing of the introduction of these submarines and missiles permits the U.S. Navy to maintain the capability of the planned sea-based component at least until 2040.

The U.S. Air Force is now upgrading strategic bombers, which implies that its current complement may be maintained through 2035 to 2045. Research and development for the next generation of heavy bombers is expected to start at the end of the next decade.

Further evidence that the United States is consistently carrying out its traditional nuclear policy is provided by the invariably steady funding, starting in fiscal year 1996, of effective programs of modernization and service-life extension for basic types of ICBMs, submarine-launched ballistic missiles, long-range cruise missiles, and nuclear bombs, as well as warhead modernization.

In accordance with the current U.S. approach, the nuclear stockpile falls into four categories. The first two categories make up the "active" arsenal. The first of these includes warheads assigned to active delivery systems, and the second includes those retrieved from delivery vehicles but kept ready for redeployment. This category also includes W-78 and W-88 nuclear warheads retrieved from Minuteman-3 and Trident-2 missiles respectively, as well as W-87 warheads from Peacekeeper MX missiles set for disassembly. The third and fourth categories of the nuclear stockpile form an "inactive" arsenal. The third category includes inactive reserve warheads that are not ready for deployment but can be used to replace warheads belonging to the active stockpile. It is thought that redeployment of the warheads of the third category would require months. The fourth category consists of the retired warheads awaiting dismantlement.

According to U.S. secretary of defense Donald Rumsfeld, some warheads removed from service are not destroyed "in case there arise some problems relating to the safety and reliability of our stored arsenal. Since we have no more operating production lines, it would be simply unreasonable for the United States to discard all these warheads and put them out of the reserve."[6]

In the goals for reduction set forth in SORT, it was stated that each party should determine the number of warheads left each year based on the results of its own periodic full assessments of military-political and technological situations in the context of national security. One of the intermediate milestones for the United States will occur at the end of 2007, when the limit of 3,800 operationally deployed warheads is expected to be achieved.

In December 2003, President Bush signed legislation passed by the Republican majority in Congress repealing a 1993 ban on research and development of low-yield nuclear weapons. The fiscal year 2004 Department of Defense budget approved by the president included initial funding for research to develop new penetration capabilities for operational nuclear weapons designed to hit hardened underground targets.

The Shifting Fortunes of Low-Yield Nuclear Weapons

In February 2003, Bush had sent Congress a letter with the administration's fiscal year 2004 budget request for the Departments of Defense and Energy in which he advocated four initiatives relating to nuclear weapons:

- Repeal of the congressionally imposed ban on research and development of low-yield (less than 5 kilotons) nuclear weapons.
- Allocation of $6 million for the Advanced Concepts Initiative, which would include research on low-yield earth-penetrating nuclear weapons.
- Allocation of $15 million for continued work on a robust nuclear earth penetrator derived from existing types of nuclear bombs and intended for use against hard and deeply buried targets.
- Allocation of $25 million for continued work toward an eighteen-month readiness posture for the Nevada Test Site. The president had issued a directive calling for the Nevada facility to acquire the capability to become ready for nuclear testing no more than eighteen months after a decision to resume such activity. The directive revoked the thirty-six-month time frame established shortly after the Cold War ended.

These initiatives provoked heated discussion, although in a very closed community of politicians and experts. Those in favor maintained that the first three initiatives added up to deterrence and thereby reduced the risk of war. As a result, they could lead to new types of nuclear weapons that would allow the United States to hit key targets in hostile countries without negatively affecting the environment, population, or friendly and allied contingents.

The problems of producing a low-yield nuclear penetrator, delivering it to a preset depth in a hard target, and developing the necessary systems of intelligence communication and target designation are extremely challenging. The penetrating weapon could not break through the obstacle deeply enough that the nuclear burst could be contained. In any case, it would produce radioactive contamination. A one-kiloton ground-penetrating nuclear warhead used on urbanized terrain would release a lethal dose of radioactive contamination over an area of a few square kilometers, killing thousands of noncombatants. Outside the urban terrain, the contamination effect would depend on wind direction, but it can hardly be expected that in selecting a location for an underground installation, the enemy would take into account the American idea of enhanced selectivity in nuclear targeting.

Democratic U.S. senators Edward Kennedy and Diane Feinstein, the most active opponents of the Bush administration initiatives, asserted that the United States was adopting "a new and dangerous plan of developing and making the next-generation nuclear weapons. How can we request Iran or Northern Korea to abandon their nuclear programs, if we have started to develop, manufacture, and test our own new nuclear weapons? . . . The new initiatives of the Bush Administration pursued in the area of nuclear weapons . . . threaten to blow up the entire architecture of verification over the nuclear weapons, which we took pains to set up over the past fifty years. We are well aware of the threats that we face in the contemporary world. It would be incorrect to add another one, treating the nuclear weapons as simply one more type of weapons in our arsenal."[7]

There is no consensus among high-ranking U.S. military officers on whether it is necessary to use nuclear weapons to destroy deeply buried targets. For instance, Admiral J. Ellis, commander of the United States Strategic Command, said during the hearing of the Senate Committee on Armed Services that the United States should reduce its dependence on nuclear weapons and use precision-guided conventional weapons instead to hit deeply buried hard targets. On May 20, 2003, Secretary of Defense Rumsfeld officially confirmed in congressional hearings that the United States intended only to study the capabilities of such a weapon, "not develop, adopt it for use, or employ it."[8]

In November 2004 Congress passed a resolution, initiated by a Republican member of the House of Representatives, David Hobson, to exclude funding for research on the low-yield penetrating charges from an appropriation for fiscal year 2005. In 2005, under growing pressure from Congress and the expert community, the Bush administration stopped the program altogether.

Is Russia Still the Focus of Deterrence?

There is no guarantee that development of low-yield penetrating charges will not be revived in the next few years. If so, as was the case with U.S. withdrawal from the ABM treaty and the onset of deployment of the BMD system, the development of a new type of nuclear warhead will be seen by the Russian strategic community as designed to threaten Russia itself.[9] The rationale for using such systems against terrorists and rogue states is unconvincing because there are alternative weapons and techniques for those purposes, so one might think that these weapons could be used to launch highly selective nuclear strikes against the hardened command centers in Russia, as well as the ICBM silos that could accommodate the bulk of Russia's nuclear forces in the future.

Such projection is absolutely inevitable, given the fact that in spite of all the declarations of politicians, the relations of mutual nuclear deterrence still exist between the United States and Russia in strategic, operational, and technical terms, with the imbalance between the parties growing stronger. Whatever American politicians and the U.S. military tell their Russian counterparts about a certain "possibility of possibilities" and the irrelevance of Cold War mutual deterrence under the new conditions, Russian specialists are well aware that Washington's reluctance to reduce its supply of warheads below the limit of 2,200 (plus approximately 1,500 warheads in reserve) cannot be explained by any strategic objective other than retention of nuclear deterrence against Russia. The grounds for sharing such a point of view are that a number of strategic warheads approximately corresponds with the number of targets for them to hit and that such a large number of targets is absent elsewhere in the world, except in Russia. Besides, the United States possesses a sufficient number of highly mobile tactical nuclear weapons to deal with any local scenario, rogue state, or terrorist entity.

There can be no other explanation for the continued U.S. structural policy of the strategic triad, with the new triad added (which does not fit within the limit of 1,000 to 1,500 warheads), other than continuation of the nuclear deterrence strategy toward Russia. The same can be said of the U.S. plan to reequip the Minuteman-3 missiles with the W-87 warheads retrieved from Peacekeeper ICBMs, as well as to continue to retain W-88 warheads aboard Trident-2 submarine-launched ballistic missiles. The W-88 is designed exclusively for fast, short-warning destruction of hardened targets, such as silo-based ICBM launchers, underground command centers, and mobile ICBMs dispersed throughout an area of routine deployment. Only Russia possesses weapons of this kind in sufficiently great numbers.

References to an indeterminate future sound like slim excuses. In any case, the United States' missile and nuclear complex surpasses that of the rest of the world many times over in terms of the rate and scale of a possible buildup of nuclear weapons in an emergency.

These aspects of the real military policy of the United States seem especially suspicious, given its efforts to dismantle the regime of nuclear arms control through its withdrawal from the ABM treaty, its reluctance to make a new large-scale treaty on strategic force reductions, its refusal to ratify the Comprehensive Test Ban Treaty, the lessening of interest in the Fissile Material Cut-off Treaty, its skepticism toward the Nuclear Non-Proliferation Treaty and the International Atomic Energy Agency, and its unilateral shift to a policy of "selective" nonproliferation and counterproliferation.

Thus, counter to Article VI of the Nuclear Non-Proliferation Treaty, the long-term nuclear policy of the United States does not seriously consider any prospect of nuclear disarmament in either military or legal aspects. What is much worse, while reducing the redundant nuclear weapons of the Cold War era, the United States displays no interest in either the material transformation of the relations of nuclear deterrence with Russia or a deepening of the agreed-upon measures of reduction and limitation of nuclear forces. Since previously manifested interest was due primarily to an apprehension of Soviet strategic capabilities, the present indifferent attitude of Washington to the issue of nuclear arms limitation cannot but be explained by the decision of Moscow to curtail its own strategic potential, and, above all, its ground-based component.

Nevertheless, the U.S. position cannot be justified, for after the Cold War ended it was the powerful United States, with a huge nuclear and conventional military "margin of safety," that could have started to radically rebuild its strategic relations with the Russian Federation, with due regard to the new risks and security challenges. Doing so would also have influenced the policy of China and other current and potential nuclear states.

Nuclear Policy of Great Britain

A Sea-Based Strategy

In pursuing its defense policy, Great Britain plans on retaining its nuclear weapons, namely the sea-based strategic nuclear forces, as a basis for national nuclear deterrence not only of traditional opponents but of certain states that have recently acquired nuclear weapons or are on the threshold of doing so.

The British nuclear forces are based on four modern nuclear-powered submarines of an indigenous design, which have become operational in the past ten years. The first boat, *Vanguard*, went to sea in December 1994; the second, *Victorious,* in December 1995; the third, *Vigilant,* in autumn 1998; and the fourth, *Vengeance,* in February 2001. Each submarine carries sixteen ballistic missile launchers. All four vessels are based in Clyde, Scotland, 32 kilometers from Glasgow.[10]

Historically, Britain's nuclear policy has been linked at many levels to that of the United States. London traditionally placed

its stake on very close cooperation with the United States, starting as long ago as World War II, and still relies on the U.S. missile early warning system. The British missiles are integrated
into the United States system of nuclear operational planning.
In October 2003, U.S. ballistic missile nuclear submarines carrying Trident-2 missiles started to be refitted with a new missile
retargeting system in accordance with the Nuclear Posture Review, the latest U.S. doctrine of strategic nuclear planning. This
will probably affect British strategic force targeting and operational planning as well.

Three-stage solid-propellant submarine-launched ballistic
missiles of Trident-2 type have been leased from the United
States and, prior to commissioning, were loaded into submarines at Kings Bay Nuclear Submarine Base in Georgia. Each
missile is fitted with a reentry vehicle housing up to eight indi-
vidually targeted warheads and ABM penetration aids. If the
latter are removed, the number of warheads can be increased to
14. The missile is accurate and delivers warheads to targets as
far as 7,400 kilometers (the range of a single-warhead Trident-2
missile is up to 12,000 kilometers). The probable circular error is
estimated at 120 meters.

With fifty-eight submarine-launched ballistic missiles carrying eight reentry vehicles each, the number of warheads aboard
four submarines could total 464. In July 1998, however, London
declared that it did not intend to have more than 200 operationally deployed warheads, thereby cutting its maximum operationally deployed stockpile by half. The cabinet announced that it
planned to keep only one ballistic missile nuclear submarine carrying 48 warheads on alert status. Therefore, each submarine carries twelve to sixteen missiles and forty warheads on average.

The thermonuclear warheads of domestic assembly have a
design and safety system similar to that of the U.S. W-76 warhead with a variable range of yields (1, 10, or 100 kilotons). The
warhead is placed in a reentry vehicle whose design is nearly
or exactly like that of the U.S. Mk-4 reentry vehicle. In supporting nuclear stockpiles and dealing with Trident missiles, Britain's
AWE Laboratory engages in close technical cooperation with
the U.S. nuclear laboratories.

Great Britain has plans for use of its nuclear weapons in two modes: a preemptive attack by all combat-ready British submarines at sea, most likely jointly with the United States; and the independent launch of a retaliatory attack from one or two British submarines while cruising in the patrol area in the northeastern Atlantic. Until recently, according to Great Britain's single integrated operational plan, up to 90 percent of British nuclear weapons were targeted primarily at military and economic targets. After Trident-2 submarine-launched ballistic missiles were adopted for use by the Royal Navy, the British could, for the first time, effectively hit strategic, hardened, fixed installations such as Russian ICBM silos and command bunkers.[11]

"First Use" Not Out of the Question

While following the United States' policy of deliberate ambiguity, the Labor government of Prime Minister Tony Blair has said that it did not rule out the first use of nuclear weapons to deter threats of use of biological or chemical weapons.[12] According to the Foreign Office, Britain, like the United States, is ready to reconsider the existing instruments for countering WMD proliferation.

In its 2003 Defense White Paper, *Delivering Security in a Changing World*,[13] the Defense Ministry crossed all the *t*s and dotted all the *i*s: Minimal nuclear deterrence by means of Trident missiles would remain an essential element of Britain's security until 2028. Given a high risk of WMD proliferation, it asserted, the existing nuclear weapons should be retained.

Still, in terms of its policy of nuclear weapon sufficiency, its attitude toward the disarmament treaties (including the Nuclear Non-Proliferation Treaty), its constructive approach toward the International Atomic Energy Agency guarantees at British facilities, and its strict position on export control, Great Britain should serve as a useful example for the other nuclear powers. This would be particularly true if some proposals of the antinuclear opposition were at some time to become a part of the official policy. The relatively constrained nuclear policy pursued by Britain, as compared to the policies of other states in the nuclear club, can be regarded largely as a result of the continuous pressure on the part of the domestic antinuclear movement. No other nuclear weapon state, whether official under the terms of the Nuclear Non-Proliferation Treaty or de facto, presently faces any serious opposition to government nuclear policy.

Nuclear Policy of France

Intimidation and Containment

Nuclear deterrence continues to play a key role in the French defense strategy. Retention of maximum freedom of choice in the deployment and use of nuclear weapons is one of the fundamental provisions of the French nuclear doctrine. The 1994 Defense White Paper, which is still in effect, says that in some cases France would not rule out preemptive nuclear strikes. However, unlike in past years, it seems that no plans are in place for strikes against opponents' cities.[14]

French military doctrine is based on the intimidation and containment strategy, according to which strategic nuclear forces are an essential element of the national armed forces. The air-based nuclear forces are regarded as a means of sending a "last warning" to an adversary about France's readiness to launch a nuclear attack.

The likely adversaries to be targeted by the French nuclear weapons are potential nuclear powers that "are capable of using their nuclear weapons against France." Another important novelty is an official acknowledgment to the effect that the French nuclear component can be integrated into the European Security and Defense Policy.[15]

According to Paris, nuclear deterrence is the best response to a likely failure of the nonproliferation policy. French president Jacques Chirac has said that French nuclear forces could cause an unacceptable amount of damage in any state that threatened France's vital national interests in any case, regardless of the threat's character or point of origin.[16]

An Emphasis on Sea and Air Basing

The French commonly suppose that nuclear deterrence should be maintained by sea-based (they prefer to call it ocean-based) and air-based strategic nuclear forces. The ocean-based strategic nuclear forces are responsible for continuity of the deterrence and, if necessary, for inflicting preplanned damage on the major enemy. The force includes four ballistic missile nuclear submarines: two Redoutable-class (S-613 *Indomptable* and S-615 *Inflexible*) and two Triomphant-class (S-615 *Triomphant* and S-617 *Téméraire*). Each submarine has sixteen launchers designed to fire solid-propellant ICBMs. Each missile is fitted with up to six multiple warheads and a set of penetration aids.

Normally, only one submarine is on alert (two in an emergency), two are stationed at their base, and one is in repair. Among them, the four missile-firing submarines deploy 48 submarine-launched ballistic missiles and 288 warheads. Reserve warheads account for 10 percent of the estimated number. After five to six years of operation, each submarine is laid up for a year-long repair of its hull, and after ten to twelve years undergoes a two-year overhaul. Each boat cruises for up to 90 days at a time.

Modernization plans are in place for as far into the future as 2015. In November 2004, France commissioned a third new ballistic missile nuclear submarine, S-618 *Le Vigilant*, armed with M45 missiles to replace the *Indomptable*. The aggregate estimated potential yield of the four boats, including a reserve of twenty-nine warheads, is 31.7 megatons.

In 2008, the last ballistic missile nuclear submarine of the old Inflexible class will be decommissioned. The introduction of a new ballistic missile nuclear submarine, S-619 *Terrible*, which was originally planned for 2008, has been shifted to July 2010. The delay is due to the development of a new submarine-launched ballistic missile that is expected to be deployed on all Triomphant-class submarines. As a result, between 2008 and 2010 the French force will consist of three missile-capable ships. After 2010, it will include four Triomphant-class ballistic missile nuclear submarines fitted with solid-propellant ICBMs.

Air-based strategic nuclear forces supplement the sea-based component. A variety of ABM penetration aids add to the deterrence, and adaptive flexibility to meet emerging threats gives French leaders new instruments of response. High maneuverability of the aircraft makes them demonstrative and deployable worldwide. In addition, the aircraft are dual capable (that is, able to deliver both nuclear and conventional weapons), which means lower procurement and maintenance costs.

All airborne delivery vehicles are organized into two units each of ground-based and sea-based aircraft. Reporting directly to the strategic air force headquarters are three squadrons of ground-based combat aircraft, a tanker squadron, a reconnaissance aircraft squadron, and a training center. Nuclear missions are assigned to 60 Mirage-2000N fighter-bombers. When refueled in the air, the aircraft can fly as far as 2,750 kilometers.

Twenty-four Super Etendard fighter-bombers (two squadrons) with a range of 650 kilometers constitute France's force of ship-based aircraft capable of carrying nuclear weapons. There is only one nuclear propulsion aircraft carrier, the *Charles de Gaulle*, which was commissioned in 2000. Another carrier (diesel powered) designed by the French is to be built at British shipyards and is expected to be commissioned by 2015, when the *Charles de Gaulle* is laid up for a total overhaul.

Starting in 2007, the focus of French air defense will be shifted from ground-based to carrier-based aircraft. There will be twenty aircraft in the ground-based component, down from the existing forty-five. Each of the two squadrons of carrier-borne aircraft will be based at its home ship, which will help increase the number of sea-based aircraft from twenty-four to forty.

France has developed nuclear weapons for penetration of opponents' BMD based on the use of antimissiles carrying nuclear warheads. France's efforts to have specific warheads and BMD penetration tactics as part of its future nuclear stockpile show that it is ready for a potential change in the military-political situation, specifically in Russia, which has a limited BMD employing antimissiles with nuclear warheads. Since there are no other states within the range of submarine-launched ballistic missiles that may have BMD in the future, this indicates that France is planning to maintain nuclear deterrence primarily against the Russian Federation through the near future despite the end of Cold War, U.S. nuclear commitments, and the unprecedented security that has blessed Europe for the last fifteen years—at least as far as traditional threats are concerned.

In June 2001, President Chirac said that French forces stationed outside the country should be protected from tactical missiles. Currently, France is working with Italy within the framework of EUROSAM (a European aerospace industrial cooperative) to develop a theater air defense system designed to intercept short-range ballistic missiles, cruise missiles, and aircraft. In addition, at the summit of NATO leaders held in Prague in November 2002, Paris confirmed its participation in a research and development program aimed at developing a European air defense system.

In implementing the program of reequipping nuclear forces, France enjoys a well-developed industry, skilled personnel, and consensus among all political parties and segments of the population.

In case the world military-political situation becomes destabilized, the French program and installations used to develop nuclear weapons can be brought back to life in a short time, including facilities for full-scale nuclear tests.[17] Over the near future Paris will pursue an active nuclear policy and maintenance of the leading role of nuclear weapons in its national military doctrine.

Nuclear Policy of the People's Republic of China

For Now, "No First Use" and Low Readiness Levels

The nuclear policy of the People's Republic of China, which has made a no-first-use commitment, is expressed in its concept of "a limited retaliatory nuclear attack." This means that the country plans to build nuclear forces that can make a potential enemy abandon the use of nuclear weapons against China through the threat of reciprocal attack. Such an approach places no value on achieving nuclear parity with developed countries, and looks quite rational in terms of material and financial resources.

The present Chinese strategic nuclear force is in a low state of readiness, and, unless additional and easily detectable steps are taken, it cannot be prepared to launch a surprise first nuclear strike. This situation is consistent with China's no-first-use concept, at least for technical reasons. Moreover, China does not have the capacity to launch even a partially disarming strike against any nuclear weapon state except India, which is usually associated with the first-use strategy. At the same time, if the Chinese strategic nuclear force were brought to a higher level of readiness in case of a crisis, China would have no alternative but a first-strike or preemptive attack because of its nuclear force's poor prospects for survivability otherwise, vulnerable command-and-control system, and weak warning system—a course of action that would be suicidal if employed against Russia or the United States. It is precisely for this reason that the Chinese strategic nuclear force has an unstable character, which would push China to a first strike and provoke a hostile preemptive attack in case of a crisis. Official declarations about no first use, motivated by ideological or political considerations, cannot change this paradoxical state of affairs. Change is made even less likely by the fact that China is a country where public discussion or independent assessment of strategic matters is virtually nonexistent. (In this sense, the difference between Russia and China is probably as big as the corresponding difference between the United States and Russia.)

There is no reason to consider China's top military leaders stupid or unprofessional and unable to comprehend the obvious nonideological strategic logic of its strategic nuclear force employment option—especially in a country famous for thousands of years of strategic thinking. China's no-first-use pledge is politically reasonable in that it averts the provocation of other great powers, but at the same time it is totally empty of strategic substance. Since China's generals must understand their first-strike predicament, as well as its suicidal consequences, there are serious reasons to expect a major modernization program of China's strategic nuclear force as soon as technical and financial conditions are right. It would be aimed at achieving a robust second-strike capability against any opponent and possibly a counterforce capability if the opportunity presented itself.

In a sense, China's current strategic posture and capabilities are quite similar to those of the Soviet Union in the early 1960s. But at that time the Cold War was in full swing (reaching its culmination in the Cuban missile crisis in October 1962), and U.S. strategic forces were also much weaker in both relative and absolute terms than the current forces of either Russia or the United States. Hence, Moscow's official declarations emphasized "the peace-loving Soviet foreign policy" at the same time that its military doctrine allowed for the possibility of a Soviet first nuclear strike "if the imperialists unleash a new world war." It was apparently assumed that an armed conflict would start in Europe and that Soviet strategic forces would be brought to top readiness and launched after NATO tactical nuclear forces were used. The Cuban missile crisis was totally different from what had been posited in the accepted strategic contingency planning and caught all sides by surprise, making them improvise and taking them to the brink of nuclear catastrophe.

One lesson of that crisis for Moscow, besides the desirability of easing tensions with Washington and agreeing on some disarmament steps, was the urgent necessity of a robust nuclear deterrent capability and parity with the United States. This led to the missile buildup of the 1960s through 1980s.

It is hard to imagine that Chinese leaders discount the possibility of an acute crisis with other great powers (around Taiwan or other issues), in which case Beijing would find itself in the situation of Moscow in October 1962. Conducting an increasingly assertive foreign policy and aiming at a global political role, China's pragmatic rulers would be naive to count only on their country's growing economic power and artful diplomacy. At the same time, they are wise and cautious enough to avoid frightening or provoking other nations or making rushed decisions or bombastic declarations regarding their nuclear force development and deployment.

China's strategic nuclear forces are variously estimated to include ground, air, and sea components, and to total 252 delivery vehicles and 300 to 400 nuclear warheads. Their base is the Strategic Missile Forces, which are equipped with 120 ground-based ballistic missile launchers. The Strategic Air Force numbers 120 obsolete H-6 (Tu-16) bombers; their production was terminated in 1994. The sea-based component consists of a single nuclear-propulsion Xia-class submarine carrying twelve launchers for Julang-1 missiles (about 1,500 kilometer range) which was launched in 1981 and is sometimes described as experimental. The substrategic nuclear forces total 150 delivery vehicles, including thirty Jian-5 tactical fighters and 120 short-range rockets. These forces are also equipped with artillery projectiles.

At present, China's strategic nuclear force is incomparably inferior to its Russian and U.S. counterparts both in quantitative and qualitative terms. China's force also lags behind those of Britain and France in a qualitative sense. Its range is restricted to the Asian Pacific, except for twenty Dong Feng-5A ICBMs with a range of 13,000 kilometers. These can reach the territory of the United States and the European part of Russia. The in-service ground-based missiles are fitted with a single reentry vehicle and placed in fixed sites such as silos and tunnels. They burn liquid fuel and take a lot of time to prepare for a launch. There is information that the nuclear reentry vehicles are stored separately from missiles to prevent an unauthorized launch.

Modernization Is under Way

China has started to deploy its first ground-mobile solid-propellant medium-range missile, the DF-21A. It is expected that within the next ten to fifteen years the country will improve its nuclear arsenal qualitatively with development of solid-propellant ground-mobile missiles with ranges of 8,000 to 12,000 kilometers, as well as new-generation ballistic missile submarines, presumably equipped with sixteen launchers each for Julang-2 missiles with a range of 8,000 kilometers. Early in 2002, series production of the solid-propellant ground-mobile DF-31 missile started at a secret plant in Sichuan Province. Its operational deployment presumably has already begun.

In ten to fifteen years, the Chinese arsenal might total 100 to 150 ground-based ICBMs, featuring high levels of readiness, technical reliability, and survivability, as well as three or four ballistic missile nuclear submarines. In 1981 China launched three earth satellites into orbit by means of a single missile, demonstrating the ability of the Chinese military-industrial complex to fit ICBMs with multiple, rather than single, reentry vehicles and BMD penetration aids.

Given the complete secrecy of the Chinese nuclear weapon program, many foreign experts involuntarily find themselves dependent on Beijing's allaying declarations, which are similar to those made by Soviet leaders in the early 1980s—the most intense years of the arms race. Besides, China's plans are compared with the past programs of the other great powers, rather than their future programs. It has been concluded that "China's participation in the nuclear race is most unlikely," and, given the fact that China currently pays great attention to economic construction and the solutions to growing socioeconomic problems, "the scale and character of the military development in China will, in the near future, be consistent with the principle of defensive sufficiency, which implies development of limited-size nuclear deterrent forces."[18]

Some American experts consider Chinese nuclear levels to be quite low, and the pace of modernization to be quite slow, which might imply a deliberate choice in favor of existential, rather than full-scale and versatile, nuclear deterrent capability.[19] This assessment has merits and is confirmed by some factual data, although China keeps all information regarding its forces and programs in total secrecy, much like the Soviet Union in the 1960s before its crash buildup. However, even if the possibility of a similar Chinese massive force deployment looks unlikely, we do not agree with the other extreme—a fully complacent view of Beijing's intentions and plans.

A closer analysis reveals, for instance, that the planned "moderate" programs of the Chinese are larger than those of any other great power. Even if China deployed only 100 to 150 ICBMs within the next ten to fifteen years, this would mean a rate of about ten missiles per year, apart from the sea-based systems. It is also probable that the mere extrapolation of the current rates of military development is a mistake. Perhaps taking into consideration the mistakes and excessive expenditures made by the Soviet Union and the United States during the Cold War, China has simply decided to skip deployment of intermediate-generation systems and is now waiting until an efficient land-mobile MIRVed ICBM system is developed, comparable to the Russian Topol-M (SS-27) missiles, before proceeding to mass production. Beijing may make the reasonable decision to terminate development of its sea-based forces—prestige systems that cannot be used effectively to deter Russia and are too vulnerable to the U.S.-Japanese antisubmarine defense to be used as a weapon against the United States. (Incidentally China may learn from Russia's current mistakes in pursuing sea-based strategic force modernization). Then, having saved a lot of money, ten to fifteen years from now China would be able to acquire 200 to 300 mobile and silo-based ICBMs of the same type. If fitted with MIRVs, they would be capable of delivering 500 to 900 nuclear warheads along all azimuths.

Thus, despite starting well behind the other great powers, China may, in the not-too-distant future, be able to seize the ripe opportunity to outrun all except the United States in leading-edge strategic nuclear force systems and take the niche of the former Soviet Union as the number-two nuclear superpower.

This assessment is fully consistent with the general framework of China's current plans of national development: playing a much bigger role in the world, resolving the Taiwan and Tibet problems, and "shifting the strategic borders beyond the national territory." Chinese leaders plan to secure for China the status of "first-rate great world power" by 2019 and, according to the information on a 1993 secret doctrine of the Communist Party of China, to overrun "three norths within the four seas," the "three norths" being Russia, NATO, and the United States.[20] The fourth sea, in addition to the Yellow Sea, East China Sea, and South China Sea, is the Sea of Japan, to which access is to be gained through the Tumangan River. This doctrine may be interpreted as indicating a determination to match or outrun Russia and the West in economic and military power on a global scale while acquiring a secure perimeter and military dominance over China's Pacific rim, directly overhanging Japan, Taiwan, the Philippines, Indochina, and Indonesia.

No Time for Complacency Toward China

There is an informed opinion in the United States that is quite complacent toward China's prospects of economic, political, and military (including nuclear force) development over the next ten to fifteen years. It is based on the concept of China's fast economic and gradual political modernization and its integration into the world (primarily Western) economic, political, and security system along the models of Japan and South Korea after 1945. This benign view has its merits and should be taken into serious account. However, a different, less optimistic perspective, one we accept, also merits consideration, if only as a hedge against unexpected dangerous developments. A recent reflections of this school of thought was presented in a *Washington Post* article by Robert Kagan, a senior associate at the Carnegie Endowment for International Peace.[21] In particular, Kagan claims that the illusion of being able to manage and integrate a rising power characterized the European attitude toward Germany after its unification under Otto von Bismarck in 1870, as well as U.S. policy toward Japan during the Meiji modernization after 1868. Both miscalculations led to world wars in the twentieth century. Kagan casts doubt on the illusion that the contemporary politicians and experts advocating a policy of "managing China" are wiser and more skillful than their predecessors of the nineteenth and twentieth centuries.

According to Kagan, the idea that China may be integrated into the East Asian security structures and the "liberal world order" overlooks the possibility that China does not intend to be integrated into a system it did not participate in creating, a system whose values run contrary to China's own traditional values and ambitions and with which China associates heavy historic grievances. Likewise, the condescending Western assessment that China is only striving toward economic growth and would not sacrifice economic ties with the West (including

Japan) for political and military gains may be an underestima-
tion. Maybe China's interest in becoming rich does not arise
from a desire to enter the world economic system, but (as was
also the case with Japan in the first half of the twentieth century) from a desire to conform that system to its own interests
and rules. The symptoms of such inclinations are clear to those
who are ready to see them: the rise of China's nationalism and
assertiveness, and its growing assuredness in its economic and
military power.

Besides, if domestic policies are any indication of China's true
values and attitude toward the use of power, then many politicians and experts in the West seem too eager to close their eyes
to the revelations of such Chinese government policies as sup-
pression of student dissent (see the Tiananmen massacre of
1989), the bloody repression of Tibetan nationalism, and the sti-
fling of any democratic developments outside the purview of
the Communist Party elite. Incidentally, such exercises of power
are not lost on the West with respect to Russia's domestic affairs, as shown by reaction to the war in Chechnya, curtailment
of democratic norms and institutions, or the Khodorkovsky trial.
These generate growing suspicion and conservatism in Western relations with Moscow, despite infinite foreign policy concessions by President Putin (a few examples are the ABM Treaty,
SORT, the war in Iraq, NATO and European Union expansion,
and elections in Georgia and Ukraine).

Indeed, in China there is no rush or crash buildup, but rather
a stable and consistent defense modernization across the whole
spectrum of conventional and nuclear forces and weapons systems. Meanwhile, these modernizations are covered by a dense
cloud of official peaceful and defensive rhetoric, appealing to
foreign strategic logical constructions and the desire for self-
deception. One example is a recent dialogue between one of the
authors of the present study and a well-versed Chinese general,
who claimed that China did not possess tactical nuclear weapons, since in any war China allegedly would only defend its
territory and would not use such weapons at home. The fact
that NATO and the Warsaw Pact claimed the same defensive

doctrines during the Cold War, but deployed thousands of tactical nuclear weapons, did not make any impression.

As for Chinese strategic nuclear forces, if they are not limited by agreements with the United States or with the United States and Russia together, the military plans and foreign policy of China will be backed up by China's great potential for nuclear missile development. In addition to the country's high rate of economic growth, another factor that is expected to substantially influence the direction of China's course is the balance of forces among Russia, the United States, China, and the rest of the Asia-Pacific region.

The long-term prospects of Sino-Russian relations cause significant, though concealed, concern in Moscow. It is possible that in 10 to 15 years, relations between Russia and China may reach a low point in their traditional cycle at exactly the same time that China enjoys maximum military superiority across the eastern Russian border, and in the world as well (in certain respects). In particular, given the maximum variant of developing its strategic forces, China would, for the first time, be able not only to launch a massive nuclear attack on the European part of Russia but to acquire considerable potential for a counterforce strike against the Russian strategic nuclear force. This could reduce Russia's capability to rely on tactical nuclear weapons in seeking to make up for the relative weakness of its general-purpose forces in the East, even for purely defensive missions.

As for relations with another great nuclear power, China is concerned about the United States' plans to set up a theater antimissile defense in Northeast Asia, as well as the prospects of U.S. support to Taiwan in this field. As long as the United States maintains large naval forces and support bases around the perimeter of the Asia-Pacific region, the security of its interests in the region is guaranteed, considering also the military contributions made by Japan, South Korea, and Taiwan. Even a supposed fast buildup of China's strategic nuclear force would affect the United States to a far lesser degree than Russia, although the novelty of such a vulnerable situation would certainly be felt acutely in Washington. If the United States BMD does not meet the expectations of its advocates, then with the expected potential of a retaliatory strike against the United States, China would rule out U.S. use of the "nuclear option" in operations against China, even if the latter posed a real threat to the United States' interests, troops, and allies in the Asia-Pacific region.

Notes

1. *Aktualnye zadachi razvitia Vooruzhennykh Sil Rossiyskoi Federatsii* [Urgent tasks of the armed forces of the Russian Federation]. (Moscow, 2003), p. 37.
2. "Voyennaya Doktrina Rossiyskoi Federatsii" [Military doctrine of the Russian Federation]. *Nezavisimaya Gazeta,* no. 74, April 22, 2000.
3. Urgent tasks, p. 42.
4. "Sud'ba RVSN" [The fate of strategic missile forces]. *Yadernaya bezopasnost* [Nuclear security], nos. 38–39 (July–August 2000).
5. "Delovaya sverka chasov" [Business watch check]. *Nezavisimaya Gazata,* March 21, 2002.
6. *Nuclear Posture Review Report* (January 8, 2002), available at www.globalsecurity.org/wmd/library/policy/dod/npr.htm.
7. *Washington Post,* April 5, 2003.
8. Alexei Arbatov and Vladimir Dvorkin, *Nuclear Deterrence and Non-proliferation.* (Moscow: Carnegie Moscow Center, 2005), p. 34.
9. "Rossiyskie strategicheskie rakety perekhvatyat nad Plesetskom" [Russian strategic missiles intercepted over Plesetsk]. *Nezavisimoye voennoe obozrenie,* no. 40 (October 22, 2004).
10. Hans M. Kristensen and Shannon N. Kyle, *Yadernye sily v mirovom masshtabe* [*Worldwide Nuclear Forces*]. SIPRI Yearbook 2003; Vooruzhenia, razoruzhenie i mezhdunarodnaya bezopasnost. Moscow, Nauka, 2004, pp. 738–741.
11. S. A. Ponomarev, "Evolyutsia voyennoy doktriny: NATO posle okonchania kholodnoy voiny [Evolution of NATO military doctrine after the Cold War]. *Strategicheskaya stabilnost,* no. 2 (2000), pp. 9–23.
12. Nicola Butler and Nigel Chamberlain, "UK nuclear collaboration with the United States." *Basic Reports,* no. 85 (March 2004), pp. 7–8, available at www.basicint.org/pubs/BReports/br85-fin.pdf.
13. Minister of Defence. 2003. *Delivering Security in a Changing World.* (Defence white paper no. Cm 6041-I). London: Ministry of Defence, available at www.mod.uk/DefenceInternet/AboutDefence/CorporatePublications/PolicyStrategy.
14. G. Fauré, *Projet de loi de finances pour 2004, adopté par l'Assemblée Nationale. Tome IV: Défense Nucléaire, espace, et services communs* [2004 finance bill adopted by the National Assembly, vol. 4, nuclear defense, space, and joint services] (Paris: Ministère de la Recherche, 2003).
15. B. Tetrais, "Nuclear Policy: France Stands Alone," *Bulletin of the Atomic Scientists,* vol. 60, no. 4 (2004), pp. 48–55.
16. G. Fauré, *Projet de loi de finances pour 2004.*

17. S. T. Brezkun, "Kritichesky analiz pozitsii Frantsii po voprosu otkaza ot yadernykh ispytany" [Critical analysis of France's position on the problem of nuclear test]. *Strategicheskaya stabilnost* [Strategic stability], no. 3 (2002), pp. 8–12.

18. P. Kamennov, "The People's Republic of China," in *Nuclear Deterrence and Non-proliferation,* ed. Alexei Arbatov and Vladimir Dvorkin (Moscow: Carnegie Moscow Center, 2005), pp. 48–54.

19. Jeffrey Lewis, "The Ambiguous Arsenal," *Bulletin of the Atomic Scientists* (May/June 2005), pp. 52–59.

20. A. Deviatov, "Pod devizom 'velichie I dostoinstvo'" [Under the slogan "Greatness and dignity"]. *Nezavisimoe voennoe obozrenie* [Independent military review], May 15, 2005, p. 6, available at http://nvo.ng.ru/wars2004-10-15/2_deviz.html.

21. Robert Kagan, "The Illusion of 'Managing China,'" *Washington Post*, May 15, 2005.

Nuclear Deterrence and Arms Control after the Cold War

A mutual nuclear deterrence relationship persists between the United States and Russia, despite their declared advance toward a "strategic partnership" in the face of new threats and challenges. Such a situation is senseless in terms of the national security of both powers because, in contrast to the decades of the Cold War, it is absurd to anticipate any armed conflict, to say nothing of a deliberate nuclear war, between the two countries. Yet mutual deterrence remains as a burdensome legacy of the nuclear arms race, and perpetuates the existence of huge nuclear stockpiles.

The Self-Generating Dynamics of the Nuclear Equation

The Strategic Offensive Reduction Treaty of 2002 (SORT) has in no way influenced the state and dynamics of mutual deterrence, which first of all should be obvious from the continued existence of strategic nuclear weapons in the available numbers and in their permanent combat-ready status. They have not been designed and deployed for any other condition than deterrence. Besides, it is precisely in this condition that nuclear weapons are continuously monitored in terms of their technical state and are most properly maintained in terms of nuclear safety.

Second, the parties involved are sure to have plans for the use of their combat-ready strategic nuclear forces, including first-strike, launch-on-warning, and retaliatory attacks against specific targets. The number of preplanned targets is of about the same order of magnitude as the number of warheads. Given the present number of warheads available to the United States and the Russian Federation, as well as the number of weapons to be eliminated by 2012 pursuant to SORT, there is no doubt that most of the targets of each of the two strategic forces are in the territory of the other country, because the majority of the targets are the sites and deployment areas of the other state's strategic and other military forces.

At least during the next ten to fifteen years, there will be no place in the whole world, besides the U.S. and Russian territories, where sufficient numbers of targets worth attacking with strategic nuclear forces could be found to accommodate the thousands of warheads on U.S. and Russian long-range missiles and bombers. The nontargeting commitment of the mid-1990s is being implemented, but it is totally unverifiable and rapidly and quietly reversible, and thus is not a serious factor in nuclear postures or war planning. In short, the sheer number of strategic weapons maintained by the United States and the Russian Federation, as well as all those planned throughout the next ten to fifteen years, inevitably and greatly contribute to mutual nuclear deterrence.

Third, it usually takes more than a decade to develop any strategic system, from elaboration of a concept and weapon design specifications to full deployment. Then, the strategic system stays in service for one or two years, or sometimes for many decades. At the same time, experience suggests that at any historical stage, political relations between two countries that are not bound together by formal military alliance, joint defense arrangements and systems, and common enemies can sharply change within a few months or weeks. In this sense, strategic planning by necessity is largely detached from current political relations as long as it is not legally constrained by international agreements on future levels, structure, deployment, combat readiness, and forms of employment of forces.

A fourth factor contributing to the organizational and technical resilience of mutual nuclear deterrence is the gigantic nuclear infrastructure that has been developed in the United States and Russia over the past few decades, and that is maintained even if at a reduced scale. This nuclear infrastructure cannot be isolated from ongoing scientific progress and technological development. This is due not only to the recognized need to preserve nuclear deterrence. Theoretically, in terms of classic deterrence the parties might decide to refrain from introducing new types of nuclear arms, but development of new technologies, information, and command systems, along with the need to enhance nuclear safety and replace fuel, guidance, navigation, and control systems, relentlessly leads to weapons upgrades. Also, nuclear laboratories and research centers would deteriorate unless engaged in improving weapon systems and use of concepts.

Fifth, and finally, the strategic nuclear balance does not exist in a vacuum—it is affected by nuclear and missile proliferation, the development of strategic defense systems and tactical nuclear weapons, changes in conventional arms and forces, and the emergence of new enemies and threats. As we have noted, even when genuinely reacting to these "external" factors, the central nuclear balance cannot but affect, often in a destabilizing way, the strategic relationship between the leading powers, at least as long as their relationship is based on mutual nuclear deterrence.

One recent demonstration of the self-generating momentum of mutual deterrence is the reported discussion of Moscow's possible withdrawal from the Intermediate and Short-Range Nuclear Forces Treaty of 1987. The first declaration to that effect was reportedly made by the minister of defense, Sergei Ivanov, during his visit to Washington in January 2005. Politically, it might be motivated by the new mood of Russian assertiveness and the perceived need to match the U.S. image of arrogance and heavy handed treatment of nuclear arms control treaties. In the strategic sense, this option may be related to the desire to enhance Russia's tactical and theater nuclear capabilities to make up for its growing conventional inferiority (exacerbated by the prospect of the extension of NATO membership to Ukraine and Georgia) and for the expected U.S. strategic nuclear and space superiority during the next ten to fifteen years. A technical consideration could be the development of medium-range conventionally armed precision-guided land-based ballistic missile systems to match the reported U.S. project to equip Trident submarine-launched ballistic missiles with conventional deep-penetrating precision-guided warheads. (Neither the Intermediate and Short-Range Nuclear Forces Treaty nor START I make a distinction between nuclear and conventional warheads on missiles of various types.)

Whatever the political and strategic merits of Moscow's initiative (which we find highly dubious), and whatever the U.S. or NATO reaction might be, it is obvious that such moves stem from the ongoing U.S.-Russian mutual deterrence relationship and that the inexorable dynamics of this relationship will again and again produce destabilizing events with negative military and political consequences for U.S.-Russian and Russian-Western relations.

This is why there is no such thing as just "maintaining" nuclear capabilities—maintenance is accompanied by a constant search for new technologies and force employment concepts. These lead to alterations in weapon systems, command-and-control capabilities, strategic concepts, and operational plans, which then affect force levels and structure because of resource availability. The changes impinge on the bilateral and multilateral nuclear balance and its stability quite apart from the evolution of political relationship between states.

Foreign and domestic political considerations may influence the nuclear balance superficially (and gradually) through the allocation of more or less funding, and sometimes in the United States (but up to now never in the Soviet Union or Russia) through direct decisions on weapon systems, operational plans, or targeting concepts. But the only way to effect significant change is through arms control treaties, which directly affect force levels and structure, and indirectly affect use strategy.

Is Arms Control Relevant Anymore?

The quasiautonomous dynamics of mutual nuclear deterrence became more pronounced in the late 1990s, and intensified further during the current decade as the START II and START III framework agreements became deadlocked in Russian and U.S. domestic and international controversies. The situation has been exacerbated because the United States' and Russian political quarters have been paying less and less attention to arms control issues in the post–Cold War military-political environment.

Attempts to make radical changes in strategic relations between Moscow and Washington simply by "assuming away" the implications of their technical and intellectual foundations did not work during the 1990s, and have been even less effective subsequently. In 2000, initial information came from sources close to the team of U.S. presidential candidate George W. Bush that the future administration intended to reject any strategic offensive arms treaty on the grounds that the era of confrontation was over and the two countries were moving toward strategic partnership. Each country was supposed to shape its own nuclear policy and program of nuclear force development independently, proceeding from its own conceptions of national security.

In Russia, this information was perceived with suspicion and displeasure. It was concluded that Washington, being aware of the critical condition of the Russian defense complex and its inability to sustain nuclear forces not only at the level of START I but also at the START II level, had decided to decisively tip the strategic nuclear balance between Russia and the United States. In this way, the United States would become the only nuclear superpower beyond the reach of any other country in the world.

At the same time, the process of agreeing on a new format for strategic relations between the two countries was hampered by a lack of clear logic in Russia's nuclear policy, which was evident in its strategic nuclear forces development program. Actually, why should there be any pragmatic motive for Washington to talk seriously with Russia about strategic arms if Moscow time and again issued statements to the effect that it could not and need not maintain nuclear parity with the United States? If the parties had switched places, Russia would probably have done the same; it would have lost interest in seriously negotiated trade-offs and solutions. An alternative approach would have required a much higher level of statesmanship in both capitals than was, and is, available.

Still, one of the serious flaws in the new U.S. position was the risk of falling into a legal vacuum. Certainly, it would be too much to agree on a new comprehensive treaty, like START I, under fully changed conditions, but a radical shift to a complete lack of a nuclear arms control regime would have brought about many unpredictable consequences, especially after the United States withdrew from the 1972 ABM treaty. Recognition of this reality on the U.S. side, and Russia's interest in having some arms control framework against the background of a new spirit of cooperation in the aftermath of the 9/11 attacks, ultimately led the parties to sign SORT in May 2002.

The basic feature of the new treaty was that it fully accommodated the previously approved U.S. and Russian plans of development of strategic nuclear forces based on their own assumptions of the military requirements and economic constraints. Thus, in contrast to START I and START II, neither country was obliged to make concessions and look for compromises that could make it adjust its plans for strategic nuclear force development. The only issues under discussion were procedures and techniques for weapons reductions, counting rules, and the associated problem of the so-called reconstitution potential (that is, an ability to build up forces to higher levels than established by the treaty ceilings).

The treaty was later criticized for including no verification measures. This charge is not quite justified, since the systems of verification and confidence-building measures defined under START I would be in effect until 2009, when START I is scheduled to go out of force. Ideally, the provisions of the verification and confidence-building measures would be extended past 2009. Moreover, as currently assumed, the verification system pursuant to START I, which includes several redundant types of monitoring, reflects in many ways the mutual mistrust of the Cold

War period. It might be simplified without reducing the actual level of transparency. Using START I, the parties would have comprehensive information about each other's forces and programs. But without warhead counting rules and procedures for weapon dismantling as applied to the provisions of SORT, this information cannot be used for verification of implementation of the new treaty.

Possibly in view of the deeply flawed Russian strategic program of 2000–2001, weak Russian diplomacy, and the conservative ideology of the Republican administration that took power in Washington in 2001, SORT was the best achievable option. Still, the fact that the new treaty does not limit any party is hardly an advantage—at least as long as the two states continue planning deployment and use of their forces largely against each other, rather than to oppose other threats separately or jointly. Profound changes in their political relations may slow nuclear modernization programs and encourage unilateral reductions of excessive force levels—but in and of themselves, such changes cannot alter the nature of the U.S.-Russian strategic relationship. Such a change requires a sustained and deeply thought-through effort on both sides with respect to military programs and negotiated agreements. The goal of this effort would be to transform the nature of strategic relations so that it was in line with new political relations. Otherwise, the old military relations would come into growing contradiction with political cooperation and might hamper or even undercut it altogether.

To do away with mutual nuclear deterrence, it is not enough just to stop being enemies. If the states retain considerable nuclear forces within range of each other, it is necessary to become full-scale military allies to achieve this goal. In this sense, the end of the Cold War in no way removed the need for new arms control agreements, but provided an opportunity for much more radical solutions with greater degrees of transparency and predictability and simpler and cheaper verification regimes. The new stage of arms control should have a new goal: instead of limiting weapon numbers and stabilizing nuclear deterrence, the new goal should be to change the very basis of the strategic relationship, liberating the maintenance of the national security of the two powers from reliance on the capability to inflict nuclear devastation on each other.

Up to now, this opportunity has been largely missed in U.S.-Russian relations after the signing of START II and START III framework treaties. SORT has not tangibly improved the situation, and looks more like lip service to nuclear disarmament than a genuine new stage of strategic arms control. (It is surely a coincidence that in Russian the abbreviation *SOR* means "trash.")

Global Partnership, Cooperative Threat Reduction, and Nuclear Deadlock

The Global Partnership program against WMD proliferation had its beginnings at the Group of Eight summit in Kananaskis, Canada, in June 2002. This arrangement may be seen as the outgrowth of cooperative efforts to eliminate WMD and nuclear materials or provide for their secure storage, in Russia and several other countries where safe management of such materials was at issue. Under the aegis of the Global Partnership, the United States and its allies (the European countries and Japan) have committed themselves to providing Russia and other post-Soviet states $20 billion over the next ten years for these tasks.

During the 1990s, a record of impressive progress toward safe elimination and storage was begun, with the most prominent effort being the Nunn-Lugar Cooperative Threat Reduction Program, which had about $6 billion throughout the decade in funding. Under this program, not only have strategic offensive weapons been eliminated per START I guidelines, but security has been enhanced in the storage and transport of nuclear materials and warheads. For instance, financial support has been given to 40,000 scientists and specialists in nuclear, chemical, biological, and missile weapons with the goal of retraining them; a large plutonium storage facility has been built in Russia; and a number of strategic nuclear submarines have been safely dismantled. Additionally, 200 tons of weapons-grade uranium acquired through the HEU-LEU (highly enriched uranium/

low-enriched uranium) U.S.-Russian project, aside from the Nunn-Lugar Program, has been used to fuel the generation of electricity at U.S. commercial nuclear power stations.

The Cooperative Threat Reduction Program was conceived as a qualitatively new type of relationship, implying cooperation in eliminating WMD and associated equipment, transcending traditional frameworks of arms control and disarmament, enhancing strategic stability at reduced levels of nuclear balance, encouraging confidence building, and creating transparency. In a sense, this new type of cooperation was perceived as analogous to a married couple jointly cleaning the room of broken dishes upon making peace after a violent quarrel. There was an expectation, at least among many of the architects of the Cooperative Threat Reduction Program, that increasingly intimate cooperation would involve openness with regard to the most sensitive military-technical systems, various cooperative industrial projects, activities on each other's territories, mutual adaptation of parts of legal systems, and massive financial transactions within the domain of defense and internal security. In the beginning, cooperation was by necessity highly asymmetric. Russia and other post-Soviet states were in a phase of deep transition and reform after the collapse of the Soviet empire and were severely short of financial and technical resources. These countries needed foreign aid themselves, and could provide little assistance to other countries. The Russian public and political elite, however, both believed in the early and mid-1990s that such a situation was temporary and that in the future Russia would be entitled to a much more equal partnership with the West.

Besides its primary purpose of transforming the political and strategic relations of the nuclear powers, the program was obviously very important for environmental safety and the cleanup of contaminated areas. Many enterprises, whole branches of defense industries, and science centers were converted from manufacturing weapons to eliminating and disposing of them. Finally, and very significantly, securing storage and transportation, as well as providing for the safe elimination of weapons and weapon-grade materials, was essential for nonproliferation of WMD and for preventing terrorists from gaining access to such weapons and materials.

Despite the great success of the Cooperative Threat Reduction Program in the 1990s, some major problems remain unresolved. About half of the nuclear weapons–grade material in Russia is still not under sufficiently reliable protection, and the safety and protection equipment of many centralized nuclear weapons storage places is still in need of modernization. Many dozens of strategic and attack nuclear submarines, withdrawn from service in Russia's Northern and Pacific Fleets, still await dismantling and remain "floating Chernobyls." Large land areas need nuclear decontamination and rehabilitation, and "nuclear cities" have not found a model of efficient economic conversion.

The Global Partnership program allows the entire set of cooperative nonproliferation endeavors to be greatly expanded and expedited over the next decade. To facilitate this, Russia has decided to enhance its financial contributions to Global Partnership projects. In 2003 and 2004, Russia allocated $300 million in each year's state budget. Specific projects were developed, which were proposed to all foreign partners. Unfortunately, the total amount of declared funding up to the present day within the Global Partnership (now embracing 22 countries) has not reached the $20 billion level established in Kananaskis. There is a significant disparity between the funds that were promised and those that have actually been allocated for projects by the participants. Russian experts point to the need to perfect the mechanisms for spending money in Russia and in the donor countries. It would also be beneficial to increase the role of audits, to evaluate the effectiveness of money spent, to use independent expertise, and to enlist Russian business to fund socially oriented projects within the framework of the Global Partnership. Russia must demonstrate an ability to perform its own tasks by itself under the Global Partnership, increasing its contribution to the funding of the projects of WMD nonproliferation and fighting international terrorism.

The lack of funding is not the only obstacle to increased international cooperation. Other key problems include questions of secrecy, bureaucracy, political restrictions, and other issues between the United States and Russia. Moscow has concentrated its efforts on settling questions of taxation, foreign access to secret nuclear sites, transparency, and liability for damage. Some of these problems were resolved in the Agreement on Multilateral Nuclear and Ecological Programs in the Russian Federation (MNEPR), signed by Russia, United States, and their European allies on May 21, 2003, and ratified by the Russian parliament later in the year.

But even the MNEPR is not addressing the fundamental problem of cooperation in the nuclear area. This problem was hidden behind legal, financial, and technical details during the 1990s and the early part of the current decade. It came out into the open only in March 2005 before the U.S.-Russian summit in Bratislava, Slovakia. It was vividly reflected in the heated discussion in the Russian State Duma and mass media of the alleged "secret agreement" between Washington and Moscow on allowing for the establishment of American control over Russian "nuclear sites and forces"[1]; the case of Evgeny Adamov, Russian minister of atomic energy from 1997 to 2001, poured more fuel on the fire. In 2005 Adamov was arrested in Switzerland at the request of the United States for allegedly stealing U.S. financial aid provided through a U.S. Department of Energy nonproliferation assistance program in the mid-1990s. Russians widely assumed that the U.S. request for the extradition of Adamov to the United States was motivated by the desire to "milk" him for the most delicate secrets of Russian nuclear weapons design.[2]

In the United States, the Adamov case stirred up opposition in Congress and the mass media to providing Russia with an ever-increasing volume of financial aid for the elimination of nuclear and chemical weapons. Behind simple accusations of misuse of money were continued concerns in some political circles about military assistance to Russia. Moscow had openly declared its nuclear forces to be the mainstay of its security, foremost through nuclear deterrence of the United States, including new strategic missiles purchased from Ukraine, produced by Russia, or developed for the purpose of overcoming a potential

U.S. BMD system. American critics of the Cooperative Threat Reduction Program questioned the wisdom of helping Russia deal with its old WMD, on the grounds that alleviating its financial burden would free up Russian financial resources for new weapons to use against the United States.[3]

On the other hand, Russia must continue with modernization of its strategic nuclear force to keep within the range permitted by SORT (1,700 to 2,200 warheads), since maintaining some strategic balance is considered essential for national security. This need is even more pressing given that the United States refused to go along with lower numbers and demonstrated a clear reluctance to devise a new full-scale arms reduction treaty in place of START I and START II/III. The combination of huge projected U.S. offensive counterforce weapons (carried by Trident-2 submarine-launched ballistic missiles and Minuteman-3 ICBMs with powerful W-87 warheads refitted from dismantled Peacekeeper MX missiles) and a strategic BMD system is commonly perceived as a technical (if not strategic) threat to Russian nuclear deterrence capability. Obliged to accept aid from the West through the Cooperative Threat Reduction Program in the past and the Global Partnership in the future, Russia is at the same time unwilling to lose its deterrence and concede clear-cut U.S. nuclear superiority, something Washington failed to retain from the 1950s to the 1980s through four big rounds of the Cold War nuclear arms race.

The dichotomy of simultaneous nuclear confrontation and nuclear cooperation was for some time unavoidable, and did not cause any serious concern in the 1990s. Consciously or subconsciously, there were hopes to remove this contradiction by enhancing cooperation while downgrading confrontation, and finally doing away with confrontation, bringing the strategic nuclear relationship in line with a political and economic partnership, with the prospect of an eventual full-scale alliance. But mutual nuclear deterrence survived and now is being projected to continue to exist, due to U.S. reluctance and Russian inability to seriously and consistently address the problems of deterrence. Instead, the problems have simply been moved to the background of the relationship and of the current official rhetoric of both countries. This has left the military and defense industrial institutions of both countries to operate unilaterally, with very little control by either the political leadership or the public.

In some areas, these deterrence-related problems have become worse through the neglect shown by state leaders, although this is not so obvious in the day-to-day political relationship between the two nations. In other areas, these problems resurface repeatedly and persist in spoiling cooperation, particularly in regard to the complex issues addressed by the Cooperative Threat Reduction Program and the Global Partnership.

It is strongly apparent that henceforth the Global Partnership will be encountering not technical obstacles but growing systemic obstacles resulting from the continued dichotomy represented by the nuclear relationship between Russia and the West. To promote cooperative nuclear (and chemical) weapons elimination projects, the United States and Russia should change their present ostrichlike attitude toward nuclear deterrence. The main task would be to elaborate and take serious steps to further reduce and stabilize the nuclear balance, and eventually, by a combination of unilateral measures and bilateral and multilateral agreements, to put it into cooperative mode in line with the concepts of cooperation of the Cooperative Threat Reduction Program and the Global Partnership.

Unlocking the Trap of Nuclear Deterrence

Attempts to change the principles of Cold War mutual nuclear deterrence between the United States and the Soviet Union (and now Russia) go back to the mid-1980s. However, all these efforts to transform the principles might be considered failures. The same is also true of a proposal to assume that post–Cold War nuclear deterrence is to be considered not as deterrence against deliberate aggression but as deterrence against a return to confrontation and the arms race. Whatever considerations may be proposed by politicians and scholars, the material basis of nuclear deterrence exists in weapons hardware and in operational planning, which implies its own logic of development, deployment, and use of nuclear forces.

It is hard to understand what role nuclear deterrence between the United States and Russia actually plays as an instrument of their military security against the background of their developing relations of partnership and cooperation (even in most sensitive areas, such as nuclear weapons safety and dismantlement). It is absurd to assume the possibility of an exchange of even single nuclear warheads, to say nothing of massive nuclear strikes. Nevertheless, deterrence can be maintained virtually indefinitely unless a set of consistent, well-thought-through, goal-oriented measures is taken.

The remaining situation of mutual nuclear deterrence between the two powers is subject to sharp criticism from various sides. It is in striking conflict not only with the proclaimed idea of a partnership, but also with that of policies on international security, nonproliferation, and counterproliferation. Whatever huge efforts are mounted at the top political level to break away from the Cold War, the situation of mutual nuclear deterrence as materialized in the military stockpiles can theoretically lead at any point to a quick restoration of the confrontation-type relations between the two powers.

Measures of a phased retreat from mutual nuclear deterrence have been developed for a long time. They include the mid-1990s agreements on nontargeting of strategic missiles against each other's territories and procedures for lowering missiles' alert status and changing submarine and bomber patrol patterns. These measures remain either symbolic or hard to implement because of the existing high quantitative levels and certain qualitative characteristics of the strategic nuclear forces of the two powers, as well as the deep-rooted plans of their combat employment, which in material terms, invariably doom Russia and the United States to oppose each other.

As an immediate objective, Moscow and Washington should turn the 2002 SORT "agreement on intentions" into a full-scale arms reduction treaty. They should agree on the stages in the weapons reductions pursuant to SORT and on the warhead counting rule. They should settle issues related to removing the secondary limitations of START I that make Russia and the United States allocate extra funds for redundant inspections, notifications, and technical changes in weapon systems. They should start discussing verification of the existence of the stored warheads and their disposal (with due regard for the successful experience of liquidation of warhead bodies under the Intermediate and Short-Range Nuclear Forces Treaty of 1987), and hold consultations on further enhancing the transparency of the strategic nuclear weapons and their operational deployment. Beyond these measures, the duration term of START I should be extended to 2012, so as not to leave an arms control and verification gap between 2009 (when START I is to end) and SORT (which should be implemented by 2012). If the legal and substantive points of SORT are fixed soon, START I extension will be needed for the sake of transparency. Finally, the duration of SORT should be extended until 2015 to avoid having the treaty expire simultaneously with the final implementation of strategic nuclear force reductions under SORT.

All of this would not, in and of itself, change the nature of U.S.-Russian strategic relations, but it would stabilize them and thus provide the necessary starting point, framework, and momentum for further steps, which would deal directly with the fundamentals of mutual nuclear deterrence.

Some may object that this would represent a return to classic Cold War arms control, allegedly irrelevant in the new environment. But this criticism does not hold water. The experience of the last decade has shown that abandoning any serious arms control effort as an anachronism of the Cold War does not remove the problems of continuous mutual nuclear deterrence, but instead leaves them uncontrolled and free to impose their self-generated effects and complications on the military and eventually the political relationships between states. In the absence of a full-scale SORT, the U.S. and Russia will have to live under the still more outdated START I. A real SORT is needed to make up for the lost time and provide the legal bridge to a different arms control that corresponds better with new military and political relations between the two leading nuclear powers.

At the next stage, it might be appropriate to conclude a SORT II, which could, for instance, provide for the reduction by 2017 of operationally deployed warheads down to the limit of 1,000 to 1,200 warheads, provided the parties agree on the appropriate definitions, counting rules, and verification.

This level is not just another lower ceiling for the same mutual deterrence potential. It is of special significance because it is apparently the lowest limit the two powers could set on their strategic nuclear forces while leaving out of the equation the nuclear forces of the three members of the Big Five, as well as ignoring the counterforce potential of long-range precision-guided conventional weapons and BMD and antiaircraft defense systems.

It is even more important that somewhere near this limit, the strategic nuclear forces of the two biggest powers cease to be targeted predominantly against each other's forces and urban-industrial sites. Taking into account the part of strategic nuclear forces that is not routinely operationally deployed, is not on patrol or on high alert, or is being overhauled or retrofitted—the combat-ready forces would then be apportioned in much more balanced ways to target each other's territories, other nuclear weapon states or rogue states, and specific targets, whether conventional or not, in other countries. Technology for quick retargeting would facilitate the assignment of strategic nuclear forces not simply to multiple attack options against each other, but multiple war scenarios against various sets of opponents. In some of those scenarios, U.S. and Russian forces might stay neutral toward each other or even act like allied forces. The nuclear balance would then be turning from predominantly bilateral to increasingly multilateral, which would start the process of unlocking the U.S. and Russian strategic nuclear forces from their traditional mutual nuclear deterrence dynamics and predicament. Besides, such a reduction would most probably make the two sides shift from triads to dyads, thus doing away with one of the most absurd legacies of the Cold War: the "nuclear overkill" mentality.

Notes

1. "Amerikansky zont nad Rossiya" [The American umbrella over Russia]. (Support Fund for Media), available at www.fondpressa.ru/press-service/analytics/detail.php?ID=902.

2. ITAR-TASS, "Adamov Should Be Extradited to Russia," September 7, 2005, available at www.tass.ru/txt/eng/level2.html?NewsID=2391110 &PageNum=0.
3. *Kommersant*, July 5, 2005. www.securities.com.

CHAPTER FIVE

Transforming the U.S.-Russian Deterrence Relationship

Reductions beyond 1,000 deployed strategic warheads seem unattractive to both Russia and the United States unless combined with stringent stability measures, which have always been controversial in view of the different geostrategic situations, force structures, and operational concepts of the two sides. At very low levels, these differences would become much more conspicuous and harder to resolve. Besides, simply making further linear reductions—down to 700, 500, or 300 warheads—would engage numerous external issues such as tactical nuclear weapons, third nuclear states, defensive systems, and conventional forces and systems. Also, if implemented within the traditional mutual deterrence paradigm, reductions to low levels could destabilize the strategic balance by making forces more vulnerable and increasing the effect of counterforce strikes. Even if that were not the case, the inexorable logic of most efficient targeting of smaller forces would place the greatest value on decapitation strikes, that is, strikes against the small number of vulnerable communications, command, control, and intelligence facilities. This would be still more destabilizing. Finally, within a mutual deterrence model, getting down to very low weapons numbers would revive the dilemma of making nuclear war less unthinkable, and deterrence less credible.

There is a frequently made argument that the very process of reducing nuclear weapons to a few hundred or dozen warheads would imply such an improvement of political relations between the parties that the related deficiencies and concerns would become irrelevant. But there is no hard proof for such an assumption. And since there may be various factors outside the strategic balance that worsen political relations, the optimistic assumption should not be taken for granted. It is believed that improvements of political relations between or among nuclear powers should not be relied upon to make up for the deficiencies in their strategic relationship. Rather, political ties should be fortified by the appropriate changes in strategic relations in specific ways and forms pertinent to such ties.

Reducing U.S. and Russian operationally deployed forces to around 1,000 warheads would avoid these negative consequences, and at the same time open the door to genuinely new steps toward revising the U.S.-Russian mutual deterrence paradigm. Those steps might start with a mutual U.S.-Russian ban on launch-on-warning operational concepts, followed by qualitatively new arms control agreements on de-alerting strategic offensive forces by technical measures and on changes in their operational deployment practices.

A Verifiable Ban on Launch-on-Warning Concepts

Although nuclear deterrence does not require the concept of launch-on-warning attacks that has been adopted by both the United States and Russia, this concept certainly implies deterrence in its most dangerous and politically least controlled form. In making a decision on launching missiles on the basis of information from early warning systems, national leaders would have only a few minutes—therefore, there is always a risk of a miscalculation or technical malfunction that could lead to accidental or inadvertent nuclear war.

Moreover, the continued practice of planning launch-on-warning attacks provides further proof that the unchanged principles of nuclear deterrence are in outrageous conflict with the partnership relations between Russia and the United States. Launch on warning refers precisely to their bilateral mutual deterrence paradigm, since only Russia and the United States have their own missile early warning systems and missiles capable of launch-on-warning strikes. This concept has nothing to do with China's nuclear forces, for its forces are not expected to have a noticeable counterforce capability in the near future. Even in the case of a hypothetical Chinese missile strike, there is no urgent incentive to launch a counterattack. The same is true of Russia's launch-on-warning operation in response to a hypothetical British or French nuclear strike, at least until the submarine-launched ballistic missile forces of Britain and France acquire counterforce capability or deliver a strike in coordination with a massive U.S. missile attack. Of course, there is always the problem of the vulnerability of U.S. and Russian communications, command, control, and intelligence systems to even a limited surprise nuclear strike, but it is generally believed that a large part of strategic force command and control could survive and be reconstituted sooner or later, with devastating retaliation the result for the aggressor.

At first sight, the rejection of the launch-on-warning concept might seem to be a purely declarative measure, with no verification provisions to back it up. Yet the rejection of launch-on-warning attack plans can be confirmed with sufficient reliability by verifiable technical means such as lowering the alert status of any component of the nuclear triad, especially the one intended primarily for missile launches based on information from warning systems.

We and experts of the Academy of Military Sciences of the Russian Federation have jointly developed a draft "Executive Agreement between the Presidents of the Russian Federation and the United States of America on Urgent Measures to Exclude the Possibility of Strategic Missile Launches on False Alarm."[1]

Under this proposed agreement, Russia and the United States would renounce plans to use strategic offensive forces in response to information originating solely from their missile early warning systems. The agreement could be cast in a form that would not necessarily require approval by the legislative bodies of the United States and Russia but could take effect upon the date of signature of the two state's chief executives. The Executive Agreement would provide for agreed-upon verifiable procedures for lowering the alert status of missiles.

Sometimes experts make proposals to immediately start lowering the readiness status of the missiles scheduled to be eliminated when warhead totals are reduced to the levels mandated by SORT (1,700 to 2,200 warheads by 2012). In our view, this might destabilize the strategic balance because modernization of the ground-based and sea-based components of the Russian strategic nuclear force is not close to being completed.

In particular, by 2012, under SORT, most of Russia's currently deployed SS-18 and SS-19 MIRVed ICBMs and SS-25 ground-mobile missiles, and all but one Typhoon and six Delta-4 ballistic missile nuclear submarines, would be decommissioned. Taking them off alert right away would leave Russia with a very vulnerable force of a few dozen silo-based SS-27 and SS-19 ICBMs, 100 to 150 SS-25 mobile missiles, and seven submarines, with only one or two at sea from time to time. The number of warheads on alert missiles would fall much lower than the SORT ceilings require. Deployment of the main force of silo-based and mobile SS-27 missiles, several ballistic missile nuclear submarines of a new class, and a new submarine-launched ballistic missile system will take many years. During this time, the existing sea-based and land-based missiles at normal alert status will be providing more force survivability, rough numerical parity, and greater stability of the strategic balance with the United States.

Since U.S. forces are sufficiently modern and efficient and are not dependent on a big modernization program to stay near the 1,700 to 2,200 SORT ceiling seven years from now, the United States does not face the same problem as Russia in the case of immediate large-scale de-alerting.

The abandonment of plans to launch missiles based on the information from early warning systems does not remove the role of these systems. They would no longer be important for urgent retaliation by the two nuclear powers against each other, but they would remain essential as long as a delayed second-strike response remained a mainstay of bilateral strategic stability (and would provide reliable information on the origin and scale of a hypothetical attack).

Simultaneously and increasingly important will be their role oriented "outward" of the bilateral nuclear balance to detect missile launches other than by Russia or the United States. The Executive Agreement would assign a special role to the Moscow-based Joint Data Exchange Center for the exchange of information derived from each party's warning systems that is based on efficient operation of the parties' early warning radars and early warning and reconnaissance satellites. These systems would play an increasing role as a means of monitoring proliferation of missiles and missile technologies, and warning of a hypothetical missile strike by a third party. Such early warning systems are sure to play still greater roles if the early warning systems of the two countries are eventually integrated. With this purpose in mind, there should be an expansion of the agreed-upon functions of the center, in addition to the expansion of its information exchange process.

It is obvious that fully or partially reduced strategic nuclear force alert status can best be maintained under conditions of profound relaxation of political and military relations, with an expanding element of cooperation. If tensions escalated in U.S.-Russian relations, the parties would most likely transfer their missiles back from low readiness to full-alert status, which could add to the level of tension, since operational and technical preparations for first and second strikes are indistinguishable. Hence, a reduced alert status per se can be considered an additional restraint on any escalation of political or military tension between the two nuclear superpowers.

Abandonment of launch-on-warning concepts may be verified in a highly reliable way by technical and operational de-alerting of strategic nuclear forces. However, before this happens, certain steps to substantiate such an agreement are necessary. One is an agreement to invite representatives of the other side to every large-scale strategic nuclear force exercise to prove that launch-on-warning training is not the purpose of the exercise. Another more far-reaching step would be to agree to place permanent liaison officers at strategic nuclear force command centers (at the U.S. Strategic Command [STRATCOM] and at Russia's Strategic Rocket Force command) as well as at the command centers of the United States' North American Air Defense Command (NORAD) and Russia's Missile-Space Defense Command. These liaison officers' service would be analogous to Russian-NATO liaison missions, with the difference being the permanent on-duty presence of foreign officers on site.

Verifiable De-Alerting of Strategic Forces[2]

Organizational and technical measures to reduce the high-alert status of strategic forces could include the following:

- agreement on a set of measures that confirm the parties' commitment to rule out the likelihood of using their strategic nuclear forces on the basis of information from missile attack warning systems.
- agreement on the stages in the process of consistent reduction of strategic nuclear forces' technical readiness for launches of ballistic missiles of various basing modes.
- implementation of organizational and technical measures that confirm the parties' commitment to rule out the likelihood of employing their strategic nuclear forces on the basis of information from missile attack warning systems.
- demonstration of the reliability of the organizational and technical measures that confirm the parties' commitment to rule out the likelihood of using their strategic nuclear forces on the basis of information from missile attack warning systems, and definition of the minimum period needed to restore the strategic nuclear forces to high readiness.
- demonstration of the feasibility of verifying the reliability of the organizational and technical measures.
- development of agreed-upon common and individual verifiable organizational and structural-technical measures to confirm that missiles cannot be launched on warning from their missile warning systems.

A major portion of the set of organizational and technical measures aimed at reducing combat readiness has already been studied by experts in the context of practical implementation of START II, which provided for "deactivation" of the delivery vehicles subject to destruction under the terms of the treaty. In doing so, these experts interpreted "deactivation" to mean that elements of the missile systems of each party should be put into a state that would make a missile launch impossible without putting these system elements back into their initial state.

Russian specialists have developed a number of alternative procedures for reducing and restoring missile launch alert status, as well as systems of inspection and notification on a changed level of combat readiness that are considered acceptable for the Russian strategic nuclear force. Most of them can also be applied to the U.S. strategic nuclear force, but they should be assessed in full detail and agreed upon by U.S. specialists.

The following methods of ICBM deactivation are feasible:

- removal of a reentry vehicle
- dismantlement of an on-board power supply unit
- dismantlement of the gas generators that open the roof of a silo launcher
- mechanical dissection of a pneumohydraulic system of ICBM prelaunch operation and firing.

The techniques of submarine-launched ballistic missile deactivation should be applied only to the ballistic missile nuclear submarines deployed at their bases. Peculiar features of submarine-launched ballistic missile deactivation are due to individual operational and technical differences between missile launches in Russia and the United States. It is commonly accepted by experts that unlike U.S. submarine-launched ballistic missiles, Russian missiles can be launched from surfaced submarines at their bases. That is why in principle they might escape an attack through launch on warning if the bases are attacked by an opponent's ICBMs or submarine-launched ballistic missiles.

Several techniques of reducing the readiness of submarine-launched ballistic missiles for immediate launch can be considered:

- obstruction of the opening of a submarine-launched ballistic missiles launcher hatch through a welding operation
- removal of reentry vehicles from submarine-launched ballistic missiles
- retrieval of submarine-launched ballistic missiles from their launchers aboard ballistic missile nuclear submarines and their placement in base storage.

In terms of economy, preference should be given to readiness-reduction measures that can be implemented at the least cost and are at the same time verifiable at a level of reliability considered acceptable by the other party.

Deactivation Techniques

Ground-Based Systems

REENTRY VEHICLE REMOVAL. When a missile is deactivated through removal of a reentry vehicle, continuing combat duty and monitoring of the missile state can be accomplished only through installation of reentry vehicle electronic substitutes (imitation devices). Removed reentry vehicles should be packed and stored in special containers at storage facilities located at ICBM bases or centralized depots.

It takes at least twenty to thirty hours to put a fixed ICBM without a reentry vehicle back on high alert, and more than thirty hours in the case of a mobile ICBM. If the reentry vehicle is stored at a central facility, the replacement time is much longer (days or weeks), since special transportation vehicles are used to take the warheads to an ICBM base.

The actions involved in downgrading high-alert status through separation of a reentry vehicle from a fixed ICBM include opening the silo protective roof, removing the missile nose cone, separating the reentry vehicle from the missile, moving the reentry vehicle to a storage site, emplacing a reentry vehicle mock-up, and closing the silo roof. To restore the high-alert status of a fixed ICBM, it is necessary to move the reentry vehicle from a storage facility to a silo and open the silo protective roof (which takes five to seven hours); remove the reentry vehicle mock-up (up to three hours); install the reentry vehicle (up to three hours); and install the nose cone, close the silo protective roof, and conduct electronic tests (ten to fifteen hours).

To reduce the missile readiness through separation of a reentry vehicle in the case of a rail-mobile ICBM, it is necessary to move an ICBM-carrying rail mobile launcher to a maintenance facility at the ICBM base, open the roof of the rail-mobile missile launcher car, hoist an ICBM container, remove the nose cone, separate the reentry vehicle, move it to the maintenance facility for storage, install a reentry vehicle mock-up, put the container with the missile down, and close the roof of the railcar.

The procedure for restoring the high readiness of a rail-mobile ICBM consists of moving the rail mobile launcher together with a missile to a maintenance facility at an ICBM base, moving the reentry vehicle from a storage facility to a rail mobile launcher, opening the roof of the railcar, and hoisting the container with an ICBM (all of which takes up to ten hours); separating the reentry vehicle mock-up (up to five hours); reinstalling the reentry vehicle (five to six hours); installing the nose cone; putting the container with the missile down into the railcar, closing the roof of the railcar, and conducting electronic tests (up to twenty hours).

To lower the high alert status of a road-mobile ICBM through reentry vehicle separation and restore it again, it is necessary to move the road-mobile launcher and a missile to a maintenance facility at an ICBM base, separate the reentry vehicle, move it to a maintenance facility at the missile base for storage, and install a reentry vehicle mock-up. The procedure for restoring the readiness of an ICBM in a road-mobile launcher includes moving the launcher together with a missile to a maintenance facility at the ICBM base, moving the reentry vehicle from a storage facility to the road-mobile launcher, and dismantling the reentry vehicle mock-up (all of which takes up to five hours); coupling the reentry vehicle (up to five hours); and conducting electronic tests (up to ten hours).

DISASSEMBLY OF AN ONBOARD POWER SUPPLY UNIT. The onboard power supply unit is used only during initial operations and while a missile is in flight. That is why disassembly of the unit does not affect the technical state of a missile when it is stored and remotely tested. Outside verification is exercised in the process of reentry vehicle separation. When an onboard power supply unit is dismantled, it is necessary to separate a reentry vehicle and emplace end caps. It takes thirty to fifty hours to restore the high readiness of a single fixed missile, and more than fifty hours in the case of a mobile ICBM.

Reduction of fixed missile readiness through disassembly of an onboard power supply unit includes several procedures, such as opening the protective roof of the silo missile launcher, separating the reentry vehicle from the missile, dismantling the onboard power supply unit, installing an onboard power supply unit mock-up, installing the reentry vehicle, and closing the roof of the launcher.

In order to restore a fixed missile's readiness, it is necessary to open the roof of the silo-based launcher (which takes five to seven hours), separate the reentry vehicle from the missile (three to five hours), dismantle the onboard power supply unit mock-up and install an actual unit (at least two to three hours), install the reentry vehicle (up to three hours), and close the roof of the silo-based launcher and conduct electronic tests (ten to fifteen hours).

Lowering the readiness level of a rail-mobile ICBM through disassembly of the onboard power supply unit entails moving the rail-mobile launcher together with a missile to a maintenance facility at an ICBM base, opening the roof of the railcar, hoisting the missile container, separating the reentry vehicle, dismantling the onboard power supply unit, installing the unit mock-up, installing the reentry vehicle, putting the missile container in the railcar, and closing the roof of the launcher railcar.

The procedure for restoring the high-alert status of a railcar-based missile entails moving the rail-mobile launcher together with the missile to a maintenance facility at an ICBM base, opening the roof of the railcar, and hoisting the missile container (all of which takes up to ten hours); separating the reentry vehicle (up to five hours); dismantling the onboard power supply unit mock-up and reinstalling the real unit (two to three hours); reinstalling the reentry vehicle (five to six hours); and putting down the missile container, closing the railcar roof, and conducting electrical tests (up to thirty hours).

Reducing the readiness of a land-based mobile ICBM through disassembly of an onboard power supply unit entails moving the road-mobile launcher together with the missile to a maintenance facility at an ICBM base, separating the reentry vehicle from the missile, dismantling the onboard power supply unit, installing an onboard power supply unit mock-up, and reinstalling the reentry vehicle. To restore the readiness of an ICBM in a road-mobile launcher, it is necessary to move the launcher together with the missile to a maintenance facility at an ICBM base and separate the reentry vehicle (which can take up to five hours); dismantle the onboard power supply unit mock-up and reinstall an actual unit (two to three hours); and reinstall the reentry vehicle (up to five hours).

DISMANTLING OF GAS GENERATORS USED TO LIFT THE PROTECTIVE ROOF. Implementation of the deactivation method requires that some additional methods of verification be worked out and that the inspection procedure be revised so that the inspection team is allowed wider access to the facility to be inspected. It takes ten to twenty hours to restore the readiness of a single ICBM.

To reduce the fixed ICBM alert status through the dismantling of gas generators used to lift the protective roof, it is necessary to carry out a sequence of five operations: enter the silo launcher, open the launcher protective roof, dismantle the gas generator, move the gas generator to a maintenance facility for storage at an ICBM base, and close the protective roof of the launcher.

To restore the alert status of the ICBM it is necessary to bring the gas generator back from the storage facility to the silo launcher, reduce the generator's combat readiness, and enter the launcher and open the protective roof of the launcher (all of which takes up to five hours); reinstall the gas generator (one hour); close the protective roof of the launcher; and conduct electrical tests (five to ten hours).

MECHANICAL DISSECTION OF PNEUMOHYDRAULICS AS AN ICBM DEACTIVATION METHOD. An ICBM can be deactivated by dismantling the pipelines (junctions) of the pneumohydraulic system for missile prelaunch operation and launching. Like other deactivation methods, this process requires that some additional methods of verification be worked out and that the procedure for inspections be revised so that the inspection team can have wider access to the installation. It takes twenty to thirty hours to restore the readiness of a single ICBM.

Sea-Based Systems

WELDING A LAUNCHER HATCH AS A MEANS OF SUBMARINE-LAUNCHED BALLISTIC MISSILE DEACTIVATION. Blocking the launcher hatch of a submarine-launched ballistic missile by means of welding requires that welding operations be conducted in each launcher, so that its hatch cannot be opened without restoration works. It takes about two hours to restore the original combat-ready status of the launcher once the hatch has been welded. This means that it would take at least twenty-five hours to restore each ballistic missile nuclear submarine to combat readiness, depending on the number of launchers and the number of welding operations. Because the launchers may or may not hold missiles, the time it would take to activate a submarine-launched ballistic missile could vary widely.

DEACTIVATION OF A SUBMARINE-LAUNCHED BALLISTIC MISSILE THROUGH REMOVAL OF REENTRY VEHICLES. Removal of reentry vehicles from submarine-launched ballistic missiles from in-base submarines as a method of reducing missile readiness requires that storage facilities be available for the removed reentry vehicles. It does not, however, demand that additional funds be allocated to keep submarine-launched ballistic missiles operational.

It takes at least three hours to replace a reentry vehicle in a submarine-launched ballistic missile. Accordingly, it will take forty-eight to seventy-two hours to replace all the reentry vehicles on a ballistic missile nuclear submarine, depending on the number of launchers on board. (In these time calculations, it was assumed that all reentry vehicles on submarine-launched ballistic missiles were located at ballistic missile nuclear submarine bases. The time required to take reentry vehicles to a base when the submarine was stationed elsewhere was not taken in account.)

DEACTIVATION OF SUBMARINE-LAUNCHED BALLISTIC MISSILES THROUGH THEIR REMOVAL FROM SUBMARINE LAUNCHERS. Deactivation of missiles by removing them from their launchers and placing them in storage facilities will result in the lengthiest process for bringing these missiles back to the required level of readiness. However, the U.S. Navy has adopted the practice of keeping some submarine-launched ballistic missiles in loading tubes, which makes it possible to load the missiles into launchers very quickly. It takes just two to four hours to load one tube-housed submarine-launched ballistic missile into a launcher, which means that loading all the launchers on an Ohio-class ballistic missile nuclear submarine will take forty-eight to ninety-six hours.

The technology for placing submarine-launched ballistic missiles in loading canisters is labor intensive and time consuming. It normally includes testing each separate stage of a missile, including its fuel quality; monitoring the assembled stages; monitoring the working efficiency of the missile, including the guidance unit and reentry vehicle; and loading a missile into a canister at a vertical assembly shop. All of these procedures together can take about 100 hours for each missile.

Even if the operations to prepare a submarine-launched ballistic missile for canister loading were run parallel to one another, it would take a long time to load the missiles, given the limited number of personnel authorized to do such work. One proposal is to limit the number of such personnel, but this technique does not seem very promising because of verification problems. It might be easier to limit the number of canisters at each base.

In the case of a full deactivation of the launcher on a ballistic missile nuclear submarine and disassembly of all submarine-launched ballistic missiles into stages, it would take about thirty days to bring a single submarine to readiness, given a sufficient amount of canisters.

The aforementioned methods allow for complete monitoring of the technical state of nuclear safety at alert status, remote electrical tests, scheduled maintenance, and technical repairs. Missile launches cannot be conducted unless restoration operations are carried out because the countdown graph is blocked automatically.

Air-Based Systems: Reduction of Bomber Readiness

The air leg of the nuclear triad is not usually associated with the launch-on-warning concept. In crises, bombers may be put on fifteen-minute alert or ordered to take off in anticipation of an attack and to stay on air patrol for many hours.

If, however, de-alerting is applied in a more general mode, bombers should also be subject to such measures. The greatest asymmetry between the United States and Russia is in the air component, and Moscow would not agree to leave it out. This is all the more so because returning missiles to high alert status may require many hours or days, and this time is in many cases shorter than the bomber flight time between the United States and the Russian Federation.

The simplest and most easily verifiable procedure for de-alerting bombers was invented for START I for the purpose of converting nuclear-capable bombers for non-nuclear missions. It consists of placing bomber nuclear weapons (air-launched cruise missiles and gravity bombs) in storage facilities no more than 100 kilometers from a bomber deployment base and prohibiting mixed basing of nuclear-capable and converted bombers.

This method seems most promising for de-alerting bombers in the context of general readiness reduction. We recommend one additional measure: prohibiting mixed basing of de-alerted heavy bombers with medium-range bombers and dual-purpose tactical strike aircraft. This would remove the need to store nuclear weapons for medium-range and tactical strike aircraft at the bases of de-alerted heavy bombers and thus compromise their de-alerting, since some weapons may be used by heavy bombers, or medium-range and tactical airplanes.

In contrast to missiles, bombers may fly to other airfields where nuclear weapons are stored and may be quickly armed to be put on high alert or take off for a nuclear strike. If this possibility is taken seriously, more complicated and expensive technical measures may be required to de-alert bombers by removing their ability to take off quickly or to carry nuclear weapons. Here, the procedures elaborated under START I for converting heavy bombers for non-nuclear missions (with functionally related observable differences incorporated) might be most appropriate. Another possibility would be to put permanent inspectors of one country at the other country's heavy bomber airbases.

Inspection Procedures for Different Deactivation

Ground-Based Systems

VERIFICATION OF THE REMOVAL OF REENTRY VEHICLES. Procedures for inspecting reentry vehicles of deployed ICBMs are described in the START I Inspection Protocol. Section 6, Article XI of the treaty specifies a quota of ten inspections per year. These procedures have been conducted more than once in practice and do not need any clarification.

VERIFICATION OF THE DISMANTLING OF THE ONBOARD POWER SUPPLY UNIT. In deactivating an ICBM by dismantling the onboard power supply unit, the fact of deactivation can be confirmed during the quota inspections conducted in conformance with Paragraph 6, Article XI of START I. Procedures for conducting inspections should be worked out in practice during their preliminary exhibition procedures and be agreed upon by the parties. During the exhibition of ICBM deactivation, the following measures may be proposed:

- Inspection procedures should be carried out with respect to the reentry vehicles of deployed ICBMs for silo launchers, rail mobile launchers, and road mobile launchers up to the moment when the reentry vehicle is separated and an ICBM and a launcher are prepared for visual examination (see Annex 3, Inspection Protocol).
- After two inspectors have made certain within one minute that the reentry vehicle has been separated, the onboard power supply unit should be prepared for a display, with some components of silo launchers, rail-mobile launchers, road-mobile launchers, and their ICBMs camouflaged.
- The upper part of the self-contained dispensing mechanism (the platform on which MIRV warheads and other elements are fixed) with an onboard power supply unit should be exhibited to the inspection teams for fifteen minutes, from a place indicated by the in-country escort, and should be photographed by the escort members using the photographic equipment of the inspected party.
- The onboard power supply unit should be dismantled and removed from the ICBM.
- For fifteen minutes, from a place indicated by the in-country escort, the inspected party should demonstrate to the inspection team that there is no onboard power supply unit aboard the ICBM, and shoot a photograph of the upper part of the self-contained dispersing mechanism minus the onboard power supply unit.

While a silo launcher, rail-mobile launcher, or road-mobile launcher, and its ICBM is being prepared for demonstration, the inspection team should be in a place or places indicated by the escort, at a distance not more than 50 meters from the silo launcher, rail-mobile launcher, or road-mobile launcher, where its members can visually and continuously observe the launcher.

PROCEDURES FOR REENTRY VEHICLE INSPECTIONS. During the postinspection procedures, it is necessary to draw up and sign an inspection report that records the fact of ICBM deactivation and includes photographs of the ICBM both with and without an onboard power supply unit. The procedure for follow-up inspections can be as follows:

- The inspectors arrive at a silo launcher, rail-mobile launcher, or road-mobile launcher they have designated for inspection.
- The inspectors compare the geographical coordinates of the silo launcher.
- From a place that has been indicated by the inspected party, the inspectors watch as the protective roof of a silo launcher (or the roof of a rail-mobile launcher) is opened and the reentry vehicle is separated.
- The inspectors confirm that the reentry vehicle has been fully separated.
- Once the ICBM is ready for exhibition, the inspection team visually examines the upper part of the self-contained dispersing mechanism for 1.5 minutes, and confirms through comparison with the photographs taken during the early exhibition that there is no onboard power supply unit there.

This method of ICBM deactivation allows the inspecting party to monitor restoration of missile readiness by its own nation's technical means of verification.

VERIFICATION OF THE DISASSEMBLY OF GAS GENERATORS USED TO LIFT THE PROTECTIVE ROOF. When an ICBM is deactivated by disassembling the gas generator that powers the lifting of the protective roof, the fact that the missile cannot be launched can be confirmed during quota inspections conducted pursuant to Paragraph 6, Article XI of START I. Procedures for conducting inspections should be tried out during early exhibitions and agreed upon by the parties.

During the early exhibition of measures to make sure that the ICBM cannot be launched, we propose that the following occur:

- The inspected party should exhibit to the inspection team, for fifteen minutes, from a place indicated by the in-country escort, where the gas generator is located, and have it photographed by escort members using photographic equipment of the inspected party.
- The inspected party should dismantle the gas generator.
- The inspected party should demonstrate to the inspection team, for fifteen minutes, from a place indicated by the in-country escort, that there is no gas generator, and should photograph the place where the generator was installed.

While the launcher is being prepared for an exhibition, the inspection team is in the place or places indicated by the escort.

During postinspection procedures, it is necessary to draw up and sign an inspection report confirming that the ICBM cannot be launched and including the annexed photographs.

The procedure for the follow-up inspections might be as follows:

- The inspectors arrive at the silo launcher that they have pointed out.
- They check the geographical coordinates of the launcher.
- They observe opening of the launcher protective roof from the place indicated by the inspected party.
- The inspection team visually examines the upper part of the silo launcher for fifteen minutes and makes sure, by comparing it with the photographs taken earlier in the exhibition, that there is no gas generator.

VERIFICATION OF THE MECHANICAL DISSECTION OF THE PNEUMOHYDRAULIC SYSTEM FOR ICBM PRELAUNCH OPERATION AND LAUNCHING. When an ICBM is deactivated through mechanical dissection of the pneumohydraulic system for prelaunch operation and launching, the fact that the missile cannot be launched might be confirmed during the quota inspections. Procedures for conducting inspections should be tried out during an early exhibition and agreed upon by the two parties.

According to this method, inspectors should be allowed access to the apparatus section of the silo launcher and inside the launcher space as deep as about 6 meters and informed about the procedure for launcher operation during a missile firing. In addition, the silo launcher and ICBM readiness can both be restored covertly, without opening the launcher protective roof. This rules out the use of the national technical means of verification (usually observation from satellites).

Sea-Based Systems: Verification of Submarine-Launched Ballistic Missile Deactivation

The variants of submarine-launched ballistic missile deactivation (for example, blocking the opening of the launcher hatch by means of welding) can be verified during inspections carried out under START I as part of the verification of the updated data. It is noteworthy that no additional measures of verification are to be agreed upon.

Verification of the Reduction of Bomber Readiness

Techniques for verifying the reduction of bomber readiness are discussed in an earlier section of the present chapter, "Air-Based Systems: Reduction of Bomber Readiness."

General Measures for Further Indicating Compliance

DEMONSTRATION OF ONGOING ORGANIZATIONAL AND TECHNICAL MEASURES. The party that chooses a particular technique for reducing missile alert status may, as a way of enhancing credibility, conduct a demonstration of the operations used to restore missile readiness, with time limits for the restoration procedures preset, and the number of items of the used special equipment (such as cranes, containers, instruments) listed. If the measures taken are not sufficiently convincing, such a demonstration becomes obligatory. Since the special equipment is normally located at facilities in support of the ICBM bases, its presence can be confirmed during inspections to verify updated data pursuant to START I. In addition to on-site inspections, information from national space systems offers additional assurance in implementing specific measures of lowering the alert status.

INFORMATION EXCHANGE. In regard to options for reducing readiness status, the information exchange implies that the following types of basic notifications should be provided:

- Notifications concerning plans to carry out specific procedures for lowering missile readiness, with the first one provided no later than three months before the demonstration procedures
- A notification concerning the date and place of exhibitions to be conducted, including a description of the procedures aimed at lowering the readiness level
- Notifications concerning the numbers of strategic offensive weapons and which measures aimed at lowering the alert status have been implemented as applied to each ICBM base or submarine-launched ballistic missile, with information about specific types of measures for the given base (no less than once every three months). As soon as the inspection team arrives at an inspected facility, inspectors are given a diagram indicating the specifics of the measures taken.

A Proposed Phased Readiness Reduction

Pursuant to SORT, each party determines for itself the structure of the forces subject to reductions. It is expedient to agree on the phases of the strategic offensive reductions to be implemented under the treaty, and, on this basis, to work out measures aimed at reducing readiness of the strategic nuclear forces that are to be affected at each of the phases.

We have developed suggestions for further measures to reduce the readiness level. First, within a reasonable amount of
time before the beginning of each phase, the parties could exchange information concerning the composition of the forces to
be reduced at a given phase. During the first three months, starting from the beginning of the new phase of reductions, the parties could implement deactivation of all strategic delivery vehicles subject to reductions at this phase through any of the
agreed-upon techniques providing for a lengthy restoration of
readiness. At the last phase, they could implement deactivation
only through the removal of reentry vehicles.

Thereafter, the parties might reach agreement that no later
than December 31, 2012, each would have no more than 500
nuclear warheads on the deployed ICBMs and submarine-
launched ballistic missiles at high alert (phase I). The next step
(phase II) would be to go down to 200 warheads on high alert
by December 31, 2015. Phase III would stipulate that in the next
few years the number of warheads ready for short-notice
launches could be reduced to 100 to 150 warheads, and eventually down to 60 to 80 for each party. This limit, however, would
largely depend on the scale and characteristics of BMD, and
still more on the profile of cooperative BMD projects, as well as
on the state of nuclear stockpiles of other countries.

The main problems, were the concept of de-alerting accepted
by the United States and Russia, would be to elaborate technical ways to ensure approximate equality between the two powers (a) as to the force numbers left on high alert at each stage
and (b) as to equality in reconstitution time of each party's strategic nuclear force. Yet another serious problem would be to
make sure that in the course of de-alerting the first strike,
counterforce capability is being downgraded more than second-
strike, retaliatory capability.

Reducing Readiness of Asymmetric Triads

It should be taken into consideration, however, that each of the
three legs of strategic triads can perform all three principle missions: first strike, launch on warning, and second strike—but at

different levels of efficiency. Silo-based ICBMs are best for a first strike and launch on warning, but less effective for a second strike. (U.S. ICBMs may become relatively more efficient for a second strike in the future in view of the degradation of Russia's counterforce capability through the withdrawal of SS-24, SS-18 and SS-19 missiles.) Mobile ICBMs are best for a second strike and launch on warning when sited in their protective shelters or at field launch positions, but not so good in a first strike. (Within a decade, all remaining Russian systems will be single-warhead or carry just a few warheads). U.S. Trident-2 submarine-launched ballistic missiles are no good for launch on warning, but would be effective in a first strike and perfect for second-strike missions. Russian present and projected submarine-launched ballistic missiles on Delta-4 and new "Dolgorukiy" class ballistic missile nuclear submarines will have limited capability in first-strike and launch-on-warning missions, while moderately good for a second strike. Heavy bombers would be no good either in a first strike (because of their long flight time) or in a second strike (because of their vulnerability while sitting at the airfields). They would be solely (and highly) efficient in launch-on-warning missions if put at a high level of takeoff readiness or on air patrol. It is true that in the case of a false alarm, bombers, unlike missiles, can be recalled. This theoretical possibility may not work in a real crisis, however. Massive takeoffs of strategic bombers may be perceived by the other side as signaling the onset of a nuclear war, and trigger the launch of its missiles. This threat may be exacerbated by the degradation of Russia's air defense system.

Hence, it is possible to suggest in a general way that the first candidates for deactivation should be silo-based ICBMs. Primary consideration might go to MIRVed ICBMs, but single-warhead silo-based missiles should be included too, in particular U.S. Minuteman-3 with counterforce W-87 warheads refitted from Peacekeeper MX missiles, since they would present a large "silo-busting" capability against Russia's 250 fixed ICBMs. Also, since land-based missiles constitute a much greater proportion of the Russian strategic nuclear force by warhead number, these missiles' large-scale deactivation should be accompanied by severe reduction of the portion of ballistic missile nuclear submarines on sea patrol and by deactivation of all or most submarine-launched ballistic missiles at bases (to prevent a quick increase in the number of submarines on sea patrol or launching ballistic missiles from bases, a Russian tactic that dates back to the Soviet era and that might be adopted in the future by the United States). Bombers should be the next priority for de-alerting, as a weapon totally dependent on launch on warning and highly provocative in such a mission. Finally, mobile single-warhead ICBMs and submarine-launched ballistic missiles with low counterforce capability should be the last to become subject to the deactivation procedure.

One additional consideration is of great importance. De-alerting strategic missiles as a way of abandoning launch on warning, as important as it is, should be implemented only as the first step in the transformation of mutual nuclear deterrence relations. This is because even without launch-on-warning concepts and weapons suitable for launch on warning, mutual nuclear deterrence may rest forever on the foundation of mutual delayed second-strike capabilities. Compared to the Cold War years and the present situation, this would be a much more stable relationship—it was the goal of arms control from the 1970s to the 1990s. Still, it would retain nuclear confrontation as its base with all the corresponding strategic, economic, and political implications. Second-strike strategic nuclear force postures would imply fully alert weapons, even though they would be *less* capable of counterforce missions or of launch on warning. Hence, further strategic nuclear force reductions plus deep de-alerting should be viewed as an instrument much likelier to effect the transformation of mutual deterrence—and eventually move both sides away from their present mutual second-strike relationship as well, actually leaving them with minimal alert strategic nuclear forces with multiple targeting plans and variable target lists across all azimuths as "a hedge against any uncertainty."

Accordingly, partial verifiable downloading of MIRVed strategic missiles (removing some of the warheads in the nose cones) would be an acceptable way of stably reducing strategic nuclear forces levels (as is envisioned under START I and apparently under SORT). This method, with appropriate counting rules and verification, could be used to reduce strategic nuclear forces down to the proposed ceiling of 1,000 to 1,200 warheads. However, de-alerting should at some point start on a parallel track, and it must deal with warheads, delivery vehicles, and launchers as a whole. For instance, it should not be possible for Russia to reach the level of 500 alert warheads by preserving 200 SS-18 and SS-19 ICBMs downgraded to one warhead each, plus 300 single-warhead SS-25 and SS-27 missiles, while de-alerting all aircraft and submarine-launched ballistic missiles. Likewise, the United States should be prohibited from reaching the 500 limit by keeping all 14 Trident ballistic missile nuclear submarines with 336 missiles downgraded to one warhead each, plus 164 Minuteman-3 ICBMs, while de-alerting 336 Minuteman-3 missiles and bombers.

Ideally, the United States' last 200 warheads remaining on alert would all be on two Trident submarines at sea (each ballistic missile downgraded to four warheads) or on one Trident at sea and 100 Minuteman-3 ICBMs. (An alternate arrangement would be fifty ICBMs and four B-2 bombers.) For Russia, such a force could comprise one "Dolgorukiy" or Delta-4 class ballistic missile nuclear submarine at sea, 30 SS-27 Topol-M missiles in silos, and 100 mobile missiles of this type. (An alternative posture could be a mix of 200 silo-based and ground-mobile SS-27 ICBMs, with all submarine-launched ballistic missiles de-alerted and one or two ballistic missile nuclear submarines with verifiable mock-up or de-activated missiles operated for training purposes.)

Since sea-based forces cannot be deactivated and de-alerted while on sea patrol, relatively deep de-alerting of strategic nuclear forces (for example, down to 500 combat-ready warheads) would lead to radical reduction of the number of U.S. Trident ballistic missile nuclear submarines at sea, from the present eight to ten down to four to five "boomers," and at a later phase, down to one or two boats. This would be a stabilizing change, given the Trident-2 missile's counterforce and counter–command-and-control strike capability. It might also induce abandonment of the traditional "two-crew" operational concept (the practice of having two full crews for each submarine to conduct more frequent sea patrols with one crew at sea while the other is resting ashore), even if some ballistic missile nuclear submarines would go to sea for exercises without ballistic missiles or with mock-up or deactivated missiles. Russia (and in the future other nuclear weapon states) would not be affected so much, since it will not maintain more than one or two boats at sea anyway. Its practice of maintaining some of its submarine-launched ballistic missile force combat ready in bases would, however, have to be stopped as well. In addition, reduction of the ballistic missile nuclear submarine patrol rate might be fixed by an agreement or through the regular exchange of data.

Ground-mobile missiles will present problems only for Russia (and in the future, possibly for China). As with submarine-launched ballistic missiles, there is not much sense in deploying mobile ICBMs "in the field" if they are deactivated. On the other hand, in their aboveground light-steel shelters ("Krona"), they are capable only of a first or launch-on-warning strike in a combat-ready state (although their counterforce capability without MIRVs is quite limited). Hence, in contrast to the case with U.S. ballistic missile nuclear submarines, at the first phase of de-alerting a reduction in the number of Russian mobile ICBMs on patrol would be destabilizing, and justifiable only by verification considerations. All declared deactivated missiles should be kept permanently in their shelters (with no first-strike or launch-on-warning capability), an arrangement that could also be formalized by an agreement.

The Issue of Reconstitution Time

Calculating and equating reconstitution time for the two sides is a complex but solvable problem. In figure 5.1, an example is provided for ICBMs at the present Russian strategic nuclear force levels. (Detailed descriptions of the technical assumptions of the modeling are provided in Appendix A.)

Figure 5.1. Reconstitution Times for De-alerted ICBMs, at 2005 Russian Force Levels

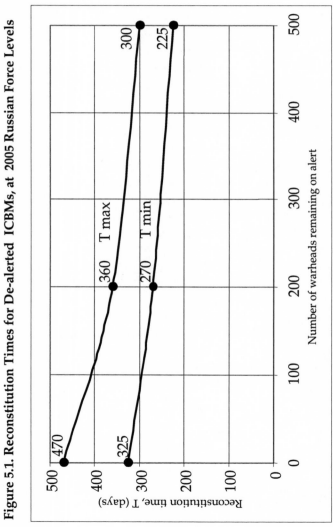

Note. ICBM, intercontinental ballistic missile.

As follows from figure 5.1, depending on the method of de-alerting and the number of missiles remaining on full alert, the reconstitution time with three shifts of support personnel (without weekends) is 225 to 470 days. With two shifts, the reconstitution time is about 30 percent longer (roughly 290 to 610 days).

Further strategic nuclear force reductions would make reconstitution time shorter because of the lower overall number of ICBMs. In figure 5.2, the model demonstrates the dependence of reconstitution time on the number of residual alert warheads and the de-activation methods for a strategic nuclear force level of about 2,000 warheads, projected by 2012 under SORT (which was enacted in 2002).

Even further reduction of the strategic nuclear force, down to 1,000 to 1,200 warheads under SORT II by 2017, as proposed in the present study, logically would imply even shorter reconstitution times, as demonstrated in figure 5.3.

This does not mean that strategic nuclear force reductions should not be implemented in order to make de-alerting less reversible. Present strategic nuclear force numbers are just too high, which would make de-alerting at the existing levels too expensive, too slow, and too technically complicated, and hence, politically more controversial. De-alerting from SORT levels (1,700 to 2,200 warheads) would be much simpler in all respects, while reconstitution time would still be quite long. Also, de-alerting from SORT would be conducive to further reductions down to 1,000 to 1,200 warheads, just by way of the dismantling of part of the de-alerted portion of strategic forces. Longer ICBM alert reconstitution time should be made up for by de-alerting of a major portion of submarine-launched ballistic missiles and heavy bombers (or conversion of the bombers to non-nuclear missions).

Most important, by the time of reduction down to 1,000 to 1,200 warheads, as suggested in the present study, strategic nuclear force reductions and de-alerting should be supplemented by integration of early warning and command-and-control systems, and eventually by development of joint BMD systems. This would make the transformation of mutual nuclear deterrence practically irreversible.

Figure 5.2. Reconstitution Times for De-alerted ICBMs (based on Russian Strategic Nuclear Force Level Projected for 2012 under the Strategic Offensive Reduction Treaty, 2002).

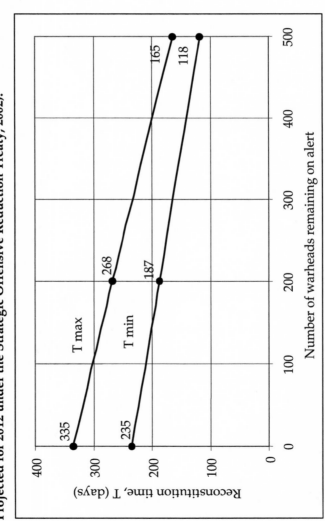

Note. ICBM, intercontinental ballistic missile.

Figure 5.3. Reconstitution Times for ICBMs (based on the Russian Strategic Nuclear Force Level in 2017 under a Proposed Strategic Offensive Reduction Treaty II)

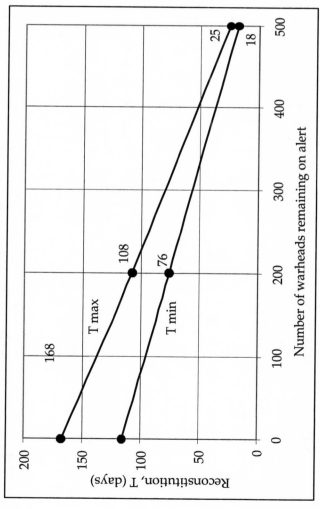

Note. ICBM, intercontinental ballistic missile.

Keeping Command-and-Control and Early Warning Intact

Survivability of command-and-control and early warning systems adds another complicated dimension to the task of moving away from launch on warning. Ensuring these systems' performance in a second strike would demand a set of special arrangements, limitations, and commitments on both sides: for example, noninterference with early warning satellites and a ban on high-orbit antisatellite systems, or a ban on deployment of ballistic missile nuclear submarines and nuclear-powered attack submarines with cruise missiles on sea patrol within 2,000 to 3,000 kilometers of each other's territories.

Accomplishing all of this would be a formidable challenge indeed. Different force structures, deployment practices, and use plans imply different deactivation techniques, which could have asymmetric effects on the two side's strategic nuclear forces. Besides, these techniques vary in implementation costs and duration, as well as in the resulting reconstitution time, cost, and visibility.

But with sufficient goodwill, such obstacles could be overcome in this post–Cold War era with no greater effort than that required to reach agreement on SALT II and START I during the Cold War. True, both nations would eventually retain a few hundred or several dozen nuclear warheads, which might be targeted at each other and at third nuclear weapon states. Still, the magnitude of de-alerting and deactivation procedures and the scale of the regime of transparency, monitoring, and limitation of operational policies would transform the mutual deterrence relationship into some new type of strategic interaction. Cooperative endeavors in early warning and defensive systems would then finish the job (see table 5.1).

Third States and Tactical Nuclear Arms

In implementing phased de-alerting of strategic nuclear forces, the United States and Russia would eventually encounter the problems posed by third nuclear weapon states and tactical nuclear forces. At sufficiently low levels of forces remaining in

Table 5.1. Phases in the Reduction of Combat Readiness of Strategic Nuclear Forces[a]

	Strategic Nuclear Warheads on ICBMs and SLBMs Ready for Launch as of the End of Each Phase[b]				
	2005	*2007*	*2010*	*2012*	*2015*
Russia	2,500	1,500	500–1,000	200–500	0–200
United States	3,000	1,500	500–1,000	200–500	0–200

Note. ICBM, intercontinental ballistic missile. SLBM, submarine-launched ballistic missile.

[a]The proposed numbers of launch-ready nuclear warheads are tentative and would have to be agreed upon by the two parties. It is probable that these numbers can be reduced to zero by common agreement. The numbers include all ICBM warheads and SLBM warheads except those on ballistic missile nuclear submarines in retrofit (four U.S. Trident submarines retrofitted for submarine-launched cruise missiles), in overhaul, or under repair at any given time (normally three Russian and two U.S.).

[b]Each phase ends on the last day of the indicated year. All years are calendar years.

combat readiness and with long reconstitution times for the rest of the forces, the two powers may become concerned, if only theoretically, about the possibility of a surprise attack by other nuclear states. Russia also might further worry about a strike by U.S. forward-based tactical nuclear weapons.

These problems could be addressed by an agreement on the part of Russia and the United States with Britain, France, and China on the expansion of de-alerting procedures to the British, French, and Chinese forces. For instance, equal ceilings could be set for the combat-ready forces of all five nuclear weapon states at a level of no more than 200 warheads. Incidentally, this solution would bypass the touchy question of equality between the two bigger and three smaller nuclear forces. The United States and the Russian Federation would retain their superiority in view of their large de-alerted forces, while the other three powers would enjoy a long-sought legalized equality with the two nuclear superpowers in combat-ready forces. The other three would legally be free to expand their de-alerted forces too, which they would hardly do for practical reasons, except for China, which probably would eventually build larger overall strategic nuclear forces (including medium-range missiles, which the two leading powers destroyed under the Intermediate and Short-Range Nuclear Forces Treaty of 1987). However, de-alerting procedures would make this Chinese buildup a less important problem. Of course, such an agreement would be easier to achieve in the context of confidence-building measures, which we address in chapter 6.

With respect to tactical nuclear weapons, de-alerting would not be applicable, since these weapons are delivered by dual-purpose systems. Hence, the solution may be an agreement to relocate all tactical nuclear weapons to central storage sites, with all such U.S. weapons being withdrawn to the continental United States. Such an agreement would not be difficult to verify through transparency measures and, if need be, permanent monitoring of the storage sites. Currently, Russia keeps tactical nuclear weapons only at air and naval bases, ready for use, and it routinely deploys them on attack submarines and surface ships at sea. All other types of tactical nuclear weapons are at central storage sites.

Since Russia's nuclear doctrine includes heavy reliance on tactical nuclear weapons in view of the relative weakness of its conventional forces facing NATO and China, such a deal on tactical weapons would still affect Russia more than other nuclear weapon states. Implementation of the Conventional Forces in Europe Adaptation Treaty by all member states would help alleviate Moscow's westward concerns. (As of April 2006, only Russia and Belarus had ratified it.) An even greater positive effect could be achieved by pursuing a new agreement on conventional armed forces in Europe, further reducing (by at least 50 percent) conventional weapon systems' national and territorial allocations under the treaty in its current form. Integrating NATO and Russian air defense systems and creating a joint interoperable rapid reaction force for enforcing and keeping the peace, conducting antiterrorist operations, and other new missions in Europe and elsewhere would go a long way toward removing the need for deployed tactical nuclear weapons to make up for allegedly inadequate Russian conventional forces capabilities. The option of keeping tactical nuclear weapons at

Figure 5.4. U.S. and Russian Deployed Strategic Nuclear Weapons On Alert and Off Alert (under the Force Reduction Proposal).

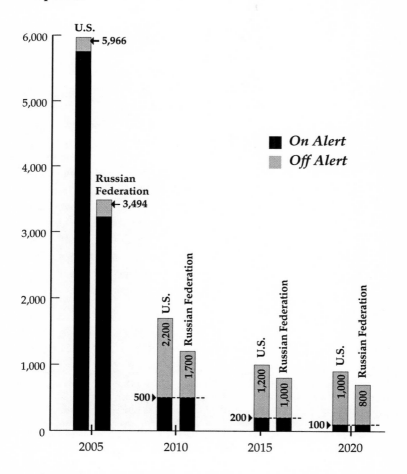

central storage sites instead of eliminating them would probably be more acceptable to Moscow as a hedge against a worst-case contingency in Europe or to Russia's east. Besides, the withdrawal of U.S. tactical nuclear weapons from Europe would be a strong incentive for Russia, and a compelling symbol of NATO's abandonment of its traditional role as a military alliance against Russia.

Indirect Benefits of De-alerting

De-alerting would indirectly lead to curtailment of the modernization programs of both strategic nuclear forces and tactical nuclear weapons, since the deployment of new systems in large numbers, to be kept mostly in a de-alerted state, would hardly make much practical sense.

Further, with a very low modernization rate and an expanding portion of the forces having been de-alerted, the size of the U.S. and Russian strategic nuclear forces would gradually decrease in a "natural" way without the need for further arms reduction agreements beyond the 1,000 warhead ceiling we call for under our proposal for a SORT II. Obsolete weapons would be withdrawn without substitute at the discretion of each side.

The numbers we call for in the reduction of overall force levels and of the de-alerted portion of strategic nuclear forces may not fully convey the sense of a qualitative change. But the steep drop in the height of the columns in figure 5.4 (as well as the increasingly close proportions of U.S. and Russian forces) illustrates in vivid spatial terms the extent of the change in U.S.-Russian strategic relations we propose. The magnitude justifiably can be said to be transformational.

Notes

1. Alexei Arbatov and Vladimir Dvorkin, *Nuclear Deterrence and Non-proliferation* (Moscow: Carnegie Moscow Center, 2005), p. 60.
2. This section borrows from a report by Vladimir Dvorkin, *Razvitie administrativnykh i technicheskikh metodov predotvrashenya puskov strategicheskikh raket po oshibke na osnovanii informatzii system preduprezhdenia o reketnom napadenii i uvelichenia vremeni prinyaniya reshenii ob otvetnikh deistviach* [*Development of Administrative and Technical Methods to Prevent Launching of Strategic Missiles by Mistake (Accident) Upon Information of Early Warning Systems and to Prolong Decision-Making Time on Retaliatory Action*] (Moscow: Strategic Nuclear Forces Center, Academy of Military Sciences, October 2004).

CHAPTER SIX

Doing away with Nuclear Deterrence

Further reduction and balanced deactivation of the U.S. and Russian strategic nuclear forces would go far beyond the task of stabilizing the nuclear balance on the principle of mutual assured second-strike retaliation, which was the conceptual core of a sequence of arms control agreements from the 1970s through the 1990s: the ABM treaty, SALT I/II, the Intermediate and Short-Range Nuclear Forces Treaty, and START I/II/III).

Deactivation would not result in the deep relaxation of the military tensions of the U.S.-Russian strategic balance (embodied in the abandonment of launch-on-warning operational concepts and the achievement of comprehensive transparency of forces, postures, and programs). It would also affect the operational policies of deployment and employment of strategic nuclear forces, thus putting the United States and the Russian Federation in a state in which they would not be able to conduct massive and coordinated nuclear strikes against each other.

Such a state would also tangibly limit their nuclear options against third nuclear weapon states or even non-nuclear opponents, all the more so if tactical nuclear weapons are also subject to de-alerting. Deep deactivation would imply a profound revision of operational deployment policies, sharply reducing ballistic missile nuclear submarine patrol rates, mobile ICBM routine dispersal drills, and heavy bomber exercises related to basing infrastructure and mission training. Under a regime of deep deactivation, making changes in these aspects of strategic nuclear force maintenance without proper notification and explanation would be equated to preparation for an act of aggression, and thus strongly deterred.

Nonetheless, even the most radical methods of de-alerting through deactivation, as much as they would move the two parties away from a combat-ready mutual deterrence relationship, would not do away with it completely. This is because such steps would remain reversible—even if only in the course of long lead times and huge expenditures of economic and organizational resources.

To make the changes related to deep deactivation irreversible, additional measures would be needed outside the realm of offensive nuclear forces: early warning and defensive systems. Gradual integration of such systems would finally and irreversibly do away with mutual nuclear deterrence, since nations with common early warning systems and missile and air defense systems technically cannot fight each other and have no reason, even theoretically, to deter each other.

Initially, nuclear and missile proliferation created the perception of a new, mutual threat, and it seemed that there would be joint interest between the United States and the Soviet Union in coping with it, and eventually a common interest among all the great powers. Common concerns about the danger of proliferation gave birth to the Nuclear Non-Proliferation Treaty and its mechanisms, and to the Missile Technology Control Regime. Dialectically, since the end of the Cold War the expanding cooperation among the great powers in fighting proliferation has raised the question of creating cooperative early warning and surveillance systems, as well as missile defense systems, that would require doing away with mutual nuclear deterrence. However, for reasons addressed in the preceding chapters, the United States and Russia, as well as the other nuclear weapon states, retained mutual nuclear deterrence as a basis of their national security strategies and as the primary mode of strategic relationships. As a result, the integration of early warning and defense systems, having barely started, gradually came to a dead end, undercutting (together with some other factors) the great powers' cooperation on nonproliferation.

To facilitate post–Cold War cooperation the great powers need to fight new security threats, and an aggressive fresh start is required in integrating early warning and defense systems. Together with the measures of reducing and de-alerting strategic nuclear forces discussed in preceding chapters, such a fresh start would finally do away with mutual nuclear deterrence and open the door to a genuine U.S.-Russian cooperative strategy for meeting the new security challenges of the twenty-first century.

Integrating Early Warning and Surveillance Systems

The best information about the proliferation of missiles and missile technologies can be obtained through an integrated effort by Russian and U.S. information and intelligence-gathering systems. As far as this mission is concerned, however, the policies of both the former and the present administrations of the United States and Russia can be characterized by a high degree of passivity and inconsistency. Apart from bureaucratic red tape and technical and political complexities, the major obstacle is not only the long-term incompatibility of such integration with the state of mutual nuclear deterrence between the U.S. and Russian strategic nuclear forces, but also the extreme lack of recognition of such incompatibility by the politicians and military establishments of both nations.

The Joint Data Exchange Center

As far back as 1998, presidents Yeltsin and Clinton made an important decision in Moscow to set up a joint center for the exchange of data from early warning systems. On June 4, 2000, representatives of Russia and the United States signed a memorandum concerning the establishment of the Joint Data Exchange

Center. This document entered into force on the date of signature and will remain effective for a ten-year period, until July 4, 2010.

The Joint Data Exchange Center is designed not only to avoid inadvertent nuclear war in case of the parties' accidental launch of missiles, but also to detect missile launches from the territories of any country and from the seas and oceans. This function is based on early warning and reconnaissance systems, and it allows for an objective verification of missile programs of other nations—above all in unstable regions such as the Middle East.

The site of the center has been chosen, and the table of organization, personnel duties, and a list of equipment have been determined. Yet the center still does not function. The superficial reasons are that the issues of taxes and damage liability have not been resolved. Resolving the problem of liability is a major task of joint U.S.-Russian nuclear threat reduction and nonproliferation projects, so there is some irony in the fact that it is the obstacle both sides have cited for the lack of project implementation in this case. Should the mutual political will develop between the two parties, this obstacle can easily be overcome without setting a precedent for other programs, because the possible damage associated with the mission of the Joint Data Exchange Center is negligible compared to the risks associated with elimination of nuclear and chemical weapons and materials.

THE BASIC MISSIONS OF THE JOINT DATA EXCHANGE CENTER. By mutual agreement, three basic missions are assigned to the Joint Data Exchange Center:

- providing information on announced and unannounced launches of ballistic missiles and space-launched vehicles detected by the Russian missile attack warning systems and the U.S. ballistic missile early warning systems
- achieving fast resolution in the Joint Commission, which provides oversight of the center, of possible ambiguous situations associated with information from early warning systems

- preparing and servicing a unified database for a multilateral regime of exchange of notifications concerning launches of ballistic missiles and space-launched vehicles.

RECOMMENDATIONS FOR MISSION EXPANSION FOR THE JOINT DATA EXCHANGE CENTER. If the Joint Data Exchange Center becomes operational, we suggest that it furnish objective displays of information about the proliferation of missiles and missile technologies. Russian missile early warning radars based near Moscow and in the newly independent states along Russia's southern border provide operational information about missile launches in regions of instability (North Africa, the Middle East, South Asia) that cannot be reached by the United States' early warning radars.

Information should be exchanged on the launches of Russian and U.S. ballistic missiles and space-launched vehicles detected by early warning systems, as well as on ballistic missile launches of third states that might pose a direct threat to Russia or the United States or might bring about an ambiguous situation and lead to its possible incorrect interpretation.

Direct transmission of data on the missile launches detected by Russian and U.S. missile early warning systems to each state's BMD system is not provided for in the agreement. Information for the Joint Data Exchange Center should be provided in a processed form, if possible, in near-real time.

Information should be exchanged for the following formats:

- When a missile launch is detected: time of launch, generic missile class, geographic area of the launch, geographic area of payload impact, estimated time of payload impact, launch azimuth
- When a launch of a space-based vehicle is detected: time of launch, generic missile class, geographic area of the launch, launch azimuth.

Accordingly, reports that launches of ballistic missiles and space-based vehicles have been detected should include these data:

- launch time
- launch location
- generic missile type: ICBM, submarine-launched ballistic missile, intermediate-range ballistic missile, medium-range ballistic missile, short-range ballistic missile, or space-launched
- launch azimuth
- impact area
- estimated time of payload impact
- indication of whether the launch was single or multiple.

The process of data exchange should be implemented in three phases. In phase I of Joint Data Exchange Center operations, information would be provided on detected launches of ICBMs and submarine-launched ballistic missiles belonging to either party and, with rare exceptions, for detected launches of space-launched vehicles also belonging to either party, including firings of ICBMs, submarine-launched ballistic missiles, and space-launched vehicles from territories of third states, as well as launches of these three types of missiles made from the territory of either party.

In phase II, it would be assumed that Russia and the United States would provide the information on detected launches included in phase I, as well as information on detected launches of other types of ballistic missiles belonging to either party with a range in excess of 1,500 kilometers or an apex altitude in excess of 500 kilometers.

In phase III, the parties would exchange information on detected missile launches specified for the two preceding phases, as well as information on launches of ballistic missiles of third states with a range in excess of 500 kilometers or an apex altitude in excess of 500 kilometers, if part of the flight trajectory of the ballistic missile as calculated by the launch azimuth was expected to go over either party's territory, or if the impact area of its payload was projected to be within either party's territory. Russia and the United States would also provide information on detected firings of space-launched vehicles of third states, if projection of the initial launch azimuth indicated an intersection of the territory of either party within the first half-orbit of launch. At its discretion, a party could provide information on other detected firings of space-launched vehicles of third states, regardless of launch azimuth.

Each party would provide information on launches of third states that it believed could create an ambiguous situation for the warning system of the other party and lead to possible misinterpretation by the other party.

Upon successful demonstration of the operational capability and procedures associated with a current phase, the heads of the Joint Data Exchange Center would jointly recommend to the Joint Commission the implementation of the next phase. Transition to the next phase would be by direction of the Joint Commission. During phase II operations, the parties would, in the Joint Commission, consider the possibility of exchanging information on missiles that intercept objects not located on the earth's surface.

In the future, Russia and the United States, in the setting of the Joint Commission, would consider the possibility of expanded data sharing on detected launches of ballistic missiles and space-launched vehicles globally, taking into account changes in the global strategic situation and the level of development of a multilateral regime for the exchange of notifications of launches of ballistic missiles and space-launched vehicles.

According to the Joint Data Exchange Center agreement, the launch information should be provided only in a processed form in accordance with an agreed-upon standard. A higher level of operational exchange might be achieved through a maximum automation of the processing of baseline information, completion of agreed-upon forms of data transfer, and presentation of the information to the center. Automating the process would allow the parties to present such information in as close to real time as possible. With this goal in mind, it could be required that agreed-upon algorithms of processing of the baseline information be developed and joint databases containing identifying images of assumed targets be set up. This would allow the center to provide the automatically processed information

in near-real time and have it confirmed subsequently by on-
duty operators at command posts of the parties' warning systems.

The Joint Data Exchange Center functions could be further
expanded through a higher level of operational data exchange
that would be the first step on the way to the permanent presence of Russian and U.S. representatives at early warning central command posts at various levels. Cooperation on the development of BMD systems discussed later in the present chapter
under "Cooperative Development and Deployment of Defensive Systems" would naturally imply expanding the center's
functions and the interlinked early warning systems with a view
to providing data to antimissile defenses.

Linking Russian and U.S. Command-and-Control

The next—and crucial—step in doing away with nuclear deterrence would be the establishment of links among strategic
nuclear force command-and-control authorities at several levels. At first it would be appropriate to develop a mobile conference and communication terminal to enable each country's
leader to have the option to be constantly in touch with his counterpart (something like the "football cases" or "nuclear suitcases"
already used by each country's head of state). Because it is sta-
tionary, the hotline that has long existed between the U.S. and
Russian leaderships is no longer enough in view of a possibility
of a third-country attack, accidental launch, or act of nuclear
terror.

Permanent direct communication links should also be established between top military authorities (the Russian defense
minister and the U.S. defense secretary, the Russian General
Staff and the U.S. Joint Chiefs of Staff) and between strategic
nuclear force commands (Russia's Strategic Rocket Force Command and the U.S. Strategic Command, or STRATCOM). This
would be important in case top political leaders became inac-
cessible at the time of a crisis for some reason. Despite all the
technical systems for political leaders' control over nuclear
forces, which are sufficiently effective in peacetime, in a crisis

situation (especially a nuclear crisis) Russian and U.S. military top commanders could still find the way to authorize the use of nuclear weapons even without political authorization if communication with the civilian head of state were lost. In such a situation, top Russian and U.S. military leaders would greatly benefit from direct communication to avoid miscalculation. Subsequently, liaison officers of the other side might be posted at these military offices (following the Russian-NATO model, but with a permanent presence).

The Joint Data Exchange Center subsequently could be used as a basis for establishing a multilateral regime of notifications and information sharing. With this end in view, after the technological infrastructure and special software were developed and some technical issues were elaborated on a bilateral U.S.-Russian basis, Russia and the United States might prepare a joint invitation to other countries to join the regime.

Putting Launch Notification on a Multilateral Basis

A multilateral regime of missile launch notifications could be set up if all the concerned states participated on a voluntary basis. In transitioning to the multilateral regime, Russia and the United States might consider placing the notification database under the supervision of an international organization such as the United Nations.

The electronic and communications architecture of the multilateral regime of missile launch notification could be based on Internet technologies, as well as equipment and software that offer rather wide access. In developing this architecture, the parties would have to pay proper attention to information security. Our proposed "International Joint Data Exchange Center" could be assigned the following tasks:

- implementation of an exchange of data on announced and unannounced missiles launches detected by the parties' warning systems
- efficient resolution of ambiguous situations related to information from warning systems of the parties

- maintenance of a unified database for notifications of missile launches
- communication of missile and space delivery launchers launch notifications to participants in the multilateral notification regime.

Involvement of other states in the notification exchange regime would expand the information base and contribute to the prevention of operational failures of missile early warning systems.

The key principle underlying the establishment of a multilateral regime of missile launch notification is the stage-by-stage accession of other states. Inasmuch as such a multilateral system is designed against miscalculation or mistaken reaction to a third-country missile launch, as well as provocative or accidental launches, and to facilitate the monitoring of missile proliferation, it does not imply political-military alliance among the parties. A major part of the technical resources would be provided by the United States and Russia, and later, possibly, by the European Union, Japan, China, and India. Other state parties would primarily be recipients of missile launch information and would provide notification of their own missile launches.

In the process of logical transition from the mere exchange of information to technical integration of larger and larger portions of early warning systems and eventually to these systems' joint development and deployment, U.S.-Russian strategic relations could not but be deeply affected, undergoing a transformation from mutual nuclear deterrence to a genuine strategic alliance (in the literal military meaning of the term *strategic*).

Cooperative Development and Deployment of Defensive Systems[1]

U.S.-Russian Cooperation on the Development and Deployment of Ballistic Missile Defenses

The final step in departing from mutual nuclear deterrence would be the transition from the joint theater BMD computer exercises of Russian and U.S. military specialists (which have been practiced for many years) to full-scale cooperation between Russia and the United States in developing and deploying BMD systems to intercept all types of ballistic missiles. This grand endeavor was conceived in the U.S.-Russian May 2002 official document *On the Foundations of Strategic Relations Between the United States of America and the Russian Federation*. Indeed, the powers that deploy and maintain a joint BMD system cannot, by definition, be opponents who deter each other with nuclear weapons. They must be full-scale military allies and be even closer than NATO or Warsaw Pact allies during Cold War times. This implies a much greater degree of commonality of foreign and security interests and policies than exists now between the United Sates and Russia, or, for that matter, even between the United States and its NATO allies (with the possible exception of Britain).

Primarily because of the remaining mutual nuclear deterrence relations and growing political controversies, nothing serious has come of the BMD cooperation agreement of 2002. Nevertheless, taking into account new threats and challenges, this may be not a totally fantastic proposition over the long term. The antimissile system, one of the major points of discord, mistrust, and hostility between Washington and Moscow in the past, might become an integrating and uniting factor in the future, fundamentally changing the political and military relationship between the two nations.

At present the parties, alternatively in Colorado Springs, Colo., and Moscow, train compatibility and coordination of tactical anti-missile systems, such as the Russian S-300 surface-to-air missile and the U.S. Patriot, in intercepting attacks of tactical ballistic missiles.

An analysis of the U.S. BMD systems presently under development shows that although full-scale research and experimental development is expected to take a long time, the participation of Russian organizations in these processes is impossible. The technical reasons are that Russian sensor technologies, element bases, and homing systems would not be attractive for use in a non-nuclear intercept. It is already too late to make use of the leading-edge Russian experience and technologies related to the high-velocity booster stages of antimissiles, for the Russian Federation has already expended huge resources on implementing the developing designs. The lost opportunities can theoretically be discussed only in regard to the booster stages of the ground-based interceptor antimissile, for their development and tests are noticeably behind those of the kill vehicle interceptors proper, and, as is known, none of the launch vehicles has yet to be tested even with a standard booster mock-up. Even if a few years ago Russia had made such an offer, however, it would have been ignored by the Pentagon, because it would have been absolutely impossible for the United States to allow the former adversary to take part in the development of the core of this strategic system. Even U.S. allies would not have been welcome to participate.

At the same time, the U.S.-developed weapons to intercept ballistic missiles at the boost phase of their trajectory have many faults that impair their effectiveness, as was specified in July 2003 by a working group of the American Physical Society.[2] According to the analysts, the missiles can be intercepted if the speed of an interceptor is more than that of the missile moving at a booster phase, and the distance between the interceptor and the targeted liquid-fueled missile is no more than 500 km (300 km for a solid-propellant missile).

The mission is still more complicated in the case of an intercept of missiles launched from the hinterland of potential threat countries. In this respect, cooperation with Russia, whose research and design organizations have an approximate ten-year lead over the United States in the technologies of high-speed interceptor missiles and solid propellants, might be very efficient at developing a new generation of BMD weapons designed to kill all types of missiles at a boost phase.

Yet this is not the only promising opportunity for cooperation between Russia and the United States. Successful interception of missiles across the full spectrum of ranges and phases of their flight largely depends on the capabilities of ground-based, space-based, and sea-based information systems. Russian phased-array missile attack early warning radar stations in

Ukraine, Azerbaijan, and Kazakhstan can provide unique capabilities to track missile launches from the "belt of instability" extending from North Africa to the Middle East, the Persian Gulf, and South Asia. Once agreements are reached on real, rather than declarative, cooperation, their incorporation into the information-gathering framework of joint BMD systems seems to be a realistic prospect.

If integrated, the capabilities of the U.S. and Russian nuclear attack warning systems would grow in terms of their efficiency. According to Bruce Blair, president of the Washington-based Center for Defense Information, the model of defense against launches of missiles from the Middle East showed that compared to the possibility of detecting missiles by means of U.S. warning systems only, a joint U.S.-Russian system would have a 20 to 70 percent higher rate of effectiveness.[3]

Much deeper cooperation can be achieved through joint deployment of the Space Tracking and Surveillance System. Spacecraft for this system, weighing around 650 kilograms each and carrying infrared and visible light sensors, are supposed to be launched into a circular orbit at an altitude of 1,350 to 1,400 kilometers and an inclination of 60 to 70 degrees. Converted heavy missiles developed under the joint Russian-Ukrainian Dnieper project would be used as launch vehicles.

The vehicle, which has a launch weight of around 210 metric tons, is a derivative of the Russian SS-18 heavy ICBM. The first and second stages of the missile are the same as those of the SS-18 missile and have not been modified. The third booster stage is a modified bus vehicle. The missile has the world's highest power performance characteristics. Some vehicles of the type converted from SS-18 ICBMs, which have been phased out because of the expiration of their service life, have proved highly reliable in commercial projects for launches of foreign spacecraft. In one launch, a vehicle carrying a booster stage and restartable engines is capable of placing two spacecraft of the STSS system into a 1,400-kilometer orbit at the required inclination. This would allow for inexpensive deployment of a constellation of low-orbit spacecraft for information support of a global BMD system.

Eventually, through the expansion of a joint BMD with land-, sea-, air-, and space-based detection, tracking, and intercept systems, the two nations could make a great contribution to the regime of missile nonproliferation. Provided that the Missile Technology Control Regime sooner or later is based on a treaty or convention, and that it envisions obligatory notification of all missile launches, such a defense system would be able to enforce this obligation by intercepting all missiles launched without notification.

Further reduction and de-alerting of strategic nuclear forces should at some point be supplemented by the integration of early warning systems and eventually of BMD systems. These second and the third avenues of cooperation, initially aimed at countering missile proliferation or a missile strike by a third party, would gradually envelop the major portion of the technical assets of the two nations, making a war between them operationally and technically impossible, and bringing them to a close strategic nuclear alliance.

Achieving Cooperation with "Third Parties"

Besides technical and strategic challenges, the prospects of close cooperation raise the touchy issue of third parties. The joint U.S.-Russian project could not leave out the two countries' close and true allies. The United States' NATO allies, Japan, and South Korea (or a unified Korea by that time) would naturally be entitled to participation and protection. Israel would certainly like to join and could also contribute quite a lot technically (since it already has been cooperating with the United States on BMD development for some time). Russian post-Soviet partners would not be a problem either, if they were politically acceptable to the West (for example, regimes in Belarus or Uzbekistan).

The real problem would emerge regarding nations with ballistic missiles or nuclear weapons (or both), such as China, India, Pakistan, Iran, North Korea (if still a rogue/failing state), Egypt, Libya, Syria, Saudi Arabia, Taiwan, Yemen, and Vietnam. If not party to a collective antimissile regime, China, India, and Pakistan would certainly perceive a multilateral and multilayered BMD system as designed to negate their nuclear deterrence and to undercut their security by making them vulnerable to and defenseless against a nuclear or conventional attack by the "members of the club." Russia is putting a high value on its political, economic, and military relations (in the last case, in the form of arms transfers) with some of the outsiders—China, India, and Iran. The United States, meanwhile, has the same attitude toward Pakistan, Egypt, Saudi Arabia, and Taiwan.

It is possible to suggest that a multilateral BMD regime should be open to third parties in its protective guarantees (although not necessarily in its development, deployment, and operational command), under certain conditions. These states would need to do away with their deterrence posture through de-alerting, deactivation, arms reductions and limitations, and transparency. They would also need to join all regimes and mechanisms of the Nuclear Non-Proliferation Treaty, Missile Technology Control Regime, Joint Data Exchange Center, and any future missile launch notification agreements. Doing away with nuclear deterrence, in particular by countries possessing relatively weak nuclear forces, would doubtlessly imply serious changes in these states' foreign policies, and possibly their domestic policies. However, it would be their choice—with the alternative being to stay out of the comprehensive framework of multilateral strategic cooperation.

Multilateral Control and Stabilization of Nuclear Arms

In the present section, only one problem is described—the possible extension of U.S. and Russian new strategic policies to other nuclear weapon states. A detailed analysis of the issues involved, including European nuclear integration, trilateral nuclear balance in the Pacific, and regional nonproliferation options, is provided in a paper published in 2005 by the Carnegie Moscow Center that was written by the two of the authors of the present study, Alexi Arbatov and Vladimir Dvorkin.[4]

The occasionally expressed idea of applying the arms control principles and negotiating techniques developed between the United States and the Soviet Union (and later Russia) to the strategic offensive arms of Great Britain, France, and China has never survived even initial scrutiny. During the Cold War, such proposals came first of all from Soviet state officials and military leaders who quite reasonably assumed that in case of a global armed conflict, the nuclear forces of the United States, Great Britain, and France would operate under a single command and target the Soviet Union—and thus should be taken into account under the ceilings and limits of nuclear arms treaties. Alternatively, the intention was to get additional concessions from the United States to make up for the larger combined forces of the West.

The United States, Britain, and France never accepted this argument. The main reason given by the British and French was that their nuclear forces were their independent deterrent, not an adjunct of the U.S. strategic nuclear force. They also claimed that Britain and France could not join the talks before their nuclear forces became comparable to those of the Soviet Union or Russia and the United States. The last argument was, and is, put forward by China as well.

At present, from a practical perspective, any attempt to mechanically include the "third" nuclear weapon states in strategic arms talks and treaties would be counterproductive. The United States and Russia can safely go down to about 1,000 strategic warheads without worrying about third nuclear weapon states. However, reducing forces to lower levels or implementing deep de-alerting through deactivation (down to 500 or 200 combat-ready warheads) would hardly be acceptable without limiting and putting under control the forces of the three smaller nuclear powers. This would be still more desirable if these nations were eventually to join multilateral early warning and antimissile defense systems and regimes.

Provided that the United States and Russia can lead the way in elaborating a new type of post–Cold War strategic arms control effort, as recommended in the present study, it might be possible by the end of this decade, in connection with a SORT II agreement, to expand partial arms limitation provisions to the forces of Britain, France, and China. As described in more detail in the Arbatov/Dvorkin CMC study,[5] French and English submarine-launched ballistic missile warheads could be limited to an equal ceiling with Russian sea-based forces in the Northern Fleet (meanwhile, in a few years, there will be no ballistic missile nuclear submarines in the Russian Pacific Fleet), and China might agree to equal ICBM ceilings with both the United States and the Russian Federation.

In the course of the deactivation and de-alerting of strategic nuclear forces, the United States and Russia might eventually involve third nuclear weapon states in agreements on equal ceilings for the remaining combat-ready strategic warheads. As pointed out at the beginning of the present section, this would help to circumvent sensitive questions on the equality of the five nuclear powers.

Confidence Building and Verification: Starting Points for Multilateral Control and Stabilization

Meanwhile, it would seem more appropriate, and easier, over the near term to reach agreements at first with Great Britain, France, and probably China, on a number of verification and confidence-building measures elaborated in START I. True, it is unlikely that these countries would agree to make full use of the treaty-defined system of such measures. First, these measures are unprecedented as regards the two nuclear powers, which have reached a high level of transparency. Such a level of transparency is not characteristic of relations even between the United States and its immediate allies. Second, many requirements of the treaty-based verification and confidence-building system are characteristic of the Cold War and currently seem redundant even as applied to U.S.-Russian relations themselves. Consequently, it seems reasonable to consider the entire system of verification and confidence-building measures in terms of whether some of the provisions may be acceptable for other nuclear powers.

The START I verification system includes sixteen types of inspections of baseline data relating to, among other things, the numbers and technical characteristics of the weapons, new missiles, and launchers under test; on-site "challenge" inspections relating to possible violations of the treaty; the number of warheads on deployed ICBMs and submarine-launched ballistic missiles; and exhibitions of new weapons.

The confidence-building measures fall into ten groups that embrace a total of 152 types of notifications. The system of information exchange between Russia and the United States envisioned by the START I Treaty includes the following:

- a biannual exchange of data on strategic offensive arms and associated facilities for all the categories of data contained in the Memorandum of Understanding on the Establishment of the Data Base
- broadcasting of all the telemetric information obtained in the course of flight and training tests of missiles, and the provision of tapes that contain a recording of such telemetric information, as well as data associated with its analysis, pursuant to the Protocol on Telemetric Information
- provision of notifications that contain the current information on the strategic offensive arms and facilities relating to them.

The goal of the treaty-defined exhibitions is to allow the other party to confirm the declared technical characteristics of the strategic nuclear arms.

Each party must conduct exhibitions to confirm

- technical characteristics of each type and each variant of ICBM and submarine-launched ballistic missile
- technical characteristics of all types of mobile ICBM launchers and variants of each type
- technical characteristics of each type and each variant of existing heavy bombers and former heavy bombers
- technical characteristics of each type and each variant of nuclear air-launched cruise missiles.

The information provided pursuant to the Memorandum of Understanding on the Establishment of the Data Base contains the following:

- quantitative data for the strategic nuclear forces, also designating their locations at bases
- technical characteristics of the strategic nuclear forces
- site diagrams of the basing locations and their support facilities
- photographs of missiles, launchers, transporter-loaders, heavy bombers, and submarines.

After each test, the party conducting the flight tests of missiles provides the other party with the following:

- tapes that contain recordings of all telemetric information broadcast during the flight test
- tapes that contain recordings of all encapsulated telemetric information, if such tapes survive
- a short description of each tape.

Additionally, after each launch, the party conducting the flight tests of missiles must provide to the other party data associated with the analysis (description of a format of the telemetry frame and techniques of encryption applied to the entire set of broadcast telemetric information, except for the information developed inside the warhead).

As far as third nuclear weapon states are concerned, all of these cooperative verification methods are neither possible nor needed. Of all inspection-based verification methods, it is possible to recommend at least two operations as universal: (a) on-site visits by foreign observers, rather than inspectors, to the exhibition of new missiles and launchers under test, and (b) a display of the number of warheads attributed to the deployed ICBMs and submarine-launched ballistic missiles.

The list of possible confidence-building measures would range much wider, and might include the following:

- the exchange of data one or two times a year concerning the quantitative characteristics of nuclear arms and associated facilities
- The provision of notifications containing the current information on nuclear arms

- advance notifications concerning test and training launches of missiles, coordinates of launch sites, and areas of reentry vehicle impact
- the provision of information concerning the new types (classes) of nuclear arms
- the provision of notifications concerning the phasing in and phasing out of nuclear arms
- the provision of information concerning dual-use delivery vehicles.

To confirm the provided information, it might be possible to agree upon the facilities and sites for an exhibition of sample nuclear weapons.

Thus, as a possible initial surrogate of multilateral nuclear arms control embracing the five great powers, it is possible to suggest an agreement or memorandum in which the nuclear arms of Great Britain, France, and China are the subject of a system of nuclear weapon transparency and confidence-building measures.

Bringing Multilateralism to States Outside the Big Five

A much more complicated problem than working with Great Britain, France, and China would be to try to involve Israel, India, and Pakistan in an expanded multilateral verification system.

The nuclear stockpiles of Israel are estimated to vary within a wide range of 50 to 200 warheads, though Israel neither acknowledges nor denies its possession of nuclear weapons. If this estimate is accurate, the maximum that can be expected is that Tel Aviv would acknowledge its possession of nuclear weapons and make a non-buildup commitment. A much more difficult problem would be to seek the prospect of Israeli nuclear disarmament in exchange for legally binding U.S. or NATO security guarantees. A precondition of such an agreement would be a guaranteed and verifiable rejection of any military or dual-purpose nuclear programs by Iran and all other states of the "Large Middle East" (including dismantlement and prohibition of any uranium enrichment or plutonium-reprocessing facilities).

After India and Pakistan declared themselves to be nuclear states, some in the expert community thought that this would contribute to a higher level of stability in the region because of mutual nuclear deterrence. However, the relation between India and Pakistan can be interpreted as an extremely unstable mutual nuclear deterrence, and the instability is chiefly due to the composition and structure of the two states' nuclear forces. The present estimate and mid-term forecast (2010 to 2015) is that India might have about 100 warheads in its nuclear forces, and Pakistan roughly half that number. The results of modeling show that India theoretically can launch a disarming attack through the use of nuclear and non-nuclear weapons that might reduce a Pakistani retaliatory strike potential to an acceptable minimum. Pakistan cannot launch a disarming attack effective enough to avert destruction of the country by Indian retaliation.

Other reasons for the instability in South Asia, as pointed out previously, are imperfect or nonexistent negative control, early warning, and reconnaissance systems, and the availability of missiles capable of carrying both nuclear and conventional warheads, which might provoke a nuclear conflict through the use of non-nuclear missiles.

Under these circumstances, the Big Five and the United Nations can be expected to take certain precautions and start initiatives aimed at forming a multistage program of stabilizing the relations between India and Pakistan. These initiatives should contain measures of confidence building and the phased reduction of tension, including measures in regard to the nuclear programs, missile tests, and recommendations on structuring nuclear forces to ensure their survivability. In the end, this could lead to agreed-upon limits on Indian and Pakistani nuclear weapons.

All of this does not mean that Israel, India, and Pakistan should be directly included in the system of multilateral nuclear arms control described in this book, or that they should be recognized as de jure nuclear weapon states as defined by the

Nuclear Non-Proliferation Treaty. These measures, along with the multilateral control within the Big Five, would, however, contribute to the strengthening of the treaty, and of global and regional stability. Besides, Israel, India, and Pakistan should be integrated into the regime through the Comprehensive Test Ban Treaty (which should be immediately ratified by the United States and China), the pending Fissile Material Cut-off Treaty, the nuclear export control regimes of the Nuclear Suppliers Group, acceptance of the International Atomic Energy Agency guarantees on declared peaceful nuclear sites, the International Atomic Energy Agency Additional Protocol of 1997, and the Missile Technology Control Regime.

It should be emphasized once more that the joint U.S. and Russian initiatives that are proposed to move away from mutual nuclear deterrence could become a good demonstration of their commitment to the disarmament objectives in Article VI of the Nuclear Non-Proliferation Treaty, and could serve as a powerful lever to impose much more stringent nonproliferation regimes on third nuclear weapon states, nuclear states outside the Nuclear Non-Proliferation Treaty, and nuclear threshold states.

Notes

1. This section borrows from Vladimir Dvorkin, "On Russian, U.S., and European cooperation on the development of missile defense," *Yadernyy Kontrol* [Nuclear control], no. 4 (74). PIR Center (2004).
2. *Report of the APS study group on boost-phase intercept systems for national missile defense* (Washington, DC: American Physical Society, July 15, 2003), available at www.aps.org/public_affairs/popa/reports/nmd03.cfm.
3. Scott Peterson, "U.S. and Russia Nukes: Still on Cold War, Hair-Trigger Alert." *Christian Science Monitor*, May 6, 2004, available at www.csmonitor.com/2004/0506/p07s01-woeu.html.
4. Alexei Arbatov and Vladimir Dvorkin, *Nuclear deterrence and non-proliferation* (Moscow: Carnegie Moscow Center, 2005).
5. Alexei Arbatov and Vladimir Dvorkin, *Nuclear deterrence and non-proliferation* (Moscow: Carnegie Moscow Center, 2005).

CHAPTER SEVEN

Conclusion

Since nuclear weapons were invented, and their horrific destructive power demonstrated in Hiroshima and Nagasaki in 1945, the least harmful way of using them has been through nuclear deterrence: the indirect use of such weapons (in the form of threats to use them) in order to prevent an enemy's nuclear aggression or large-scale conventional attack.

At the same time, having allegedly proved its utility in advancing individual states' national security and foreign policy, nuclear deterrence could not help but give birth to nuclear proliferation, since more and more states developed an interest and technical-economic capacity to join the elite "nuclear club."

Thirteen countries (counting North Korea) have acquired nuclear weapons since 1945. Four have since relinquished them (Belarus, Kazakhstan, South Africa, and Ukraine). About a dozen more have pursued military nuclear programs in the past or are suspected of doing so now. A dialectic continuation of this process in an era of globalization and the information revolution eventually leads to substate entities, foremost terrorist organizations, gaining access to nuclear weapons, and using them to blackmail or destroy the civilized world.

The technological revolution, with its development of low-yield and selective-effect nuclear munitions, dual-purpose delivery vehicles, antimissile defense systems, and space-based and precision-guided conventional weapons, has resulted in the erosion of nuclear deterrence from the other end—technical innovations of the most advanced states blurring the "nuclear threshold."

As nuclear deterrence and its means become more multilateral, uneven in their technical foundations, and eventually available to substate entities, nuclear deterrence will become more and more precarious as the basis of the security and foreign policy of the great powers. As a strategy for avoiding nuclear war while possessing many nuclear arms, nuclear deterrence thus bears the seeds of its own eventual failure through the eruption of actual nuclear warfare. The question is not "whether," but "when and how."

What is most amazing is that all of these dangerous political and technical developments are happening (or are forecast to happen) after the end of the Cold War, which was directly associated with nuclear deterrence and perceptions of the highest threat of actual nuclear war. The end of the Cold War, in a sense, played a bad joke on the antinuclear aspirations of humankind: No longer terrified by the prospect of the escalation of certain conflicts to nuclear holocaust, the leading nuclear powers now emphasize actual nuclear warfare instead of deterrence. They plan for preemptive nuclear strikes and combined operations of nuclear and conventional systems in both offensive and defensive missions. In response to this, or using this as a convenient pretext, some third nuclear weapon states and threshold regimes treat nuclear weapons as the only means of deterring the great powers. Meanwhile, these aspirations open more channels for terrorists to gain access to nuclear explosives.

New security challenges are piling up. Among many others, they include the proliferation of missiles, nuclear arms, and other means of mass destruction; international terrorism; ethnic and religious conflicts with transborder repercussions; the subversive role of "rogue" and "failed states"; and inadequate accounting for nuclear stockpiles in many countries of the world. There is no doubt that these problems can be addressed only through broad and genuine cooperation among the great powers and other economically and politically successful nations. We firmly believe that neither the United States and Russia alone, nor all five great powers working together, will be able to cooperate effectively and consistently on security as long as they retain and refine the thousands of nuclear weapons that, while designed for mutual destruction, are somehow designated the material foundation of mutual nuclear deterrence.

It is now an established fact of life, demonstrated by the recent fifteen-year political experience that without a well-conceived, long-term, persistent joint effort that combines diplomacy, finances, technology, and politics in a new type of arms control endeavor, mutual nuclear deterrence will not take care of itself and fade away—even though the political and ideological foundations of deterrence have become history along with the Cold War.

As long as nuclear weapons exist, nuclear deterrence, proliferation, and even the actual use of such weapons cannot be discounted. Only the full elimination of nuclear weapons, final and complete nuclear disarmament, might provide a guarantee against this eventuality. However, first, it is not at all clear what the strategic and technical meaning of the term "nuclear disarmament" is. Second, nuclear disarmament could have the unfortunate effects of making the world "safe" for large-scale conventional wars, or for the use of other WMD or new classes of weapons. Hence, the very threat of force and use of force, as the primary instrument of international relations for thousands of years, will have to be fully revised—which will lead to some kind of world supranational government (besides the creation of an international nuclear energy complex or world energy corporation). Such a project is not easy to contemplate theoretically, to say nothing of its practical implementation. And it goes far beyond the scope of the present study.

As for the present book, its focal point is the fundamental dilemma for the present time and the near future: Is it possible for the United States and the Russian Federation to do away with mutual nuclear deterrence while (1) retaining hundreds or thousands of nuclear weapons and (2) lacking "a clear and present" common enemy strong enough for the two nations to unite against with their combined nuclear arsenals?

Based on the analysis we have presented, we think that it is possible, provided that sufficient political will, intellectual resources, and administrative efforts are applied to this goal by the United States and Russia, and later by the other great powers.

By way of reservation, it is necessary to point out that since many nuclear weapons would regardless remain in service and storage, even if our recommendations became reality, nuclear deterrence will still remain a remote possibility among the states that implement such proposals. Also, in a more practical operational and technical form, nuclear deterrence would be preserved for the states that did not enter into this new type of nuclear nondeterrence relationship.

What is most important, however, is that mutual nuclear deterrence be removed (1) as the foundation of the operational strategic relationship between Russia and the United States, (2) as the material embodiment of the two states' confrontational military relations, (3) as an impediment to their security and political cooperation against new threats, and (4) as a huge drain on their financial resources and scientific-technological innovations. Toward this end, we propose a sequence of nine steps, to be taken bilaterally by Russia and the United States (see Appendix A for a diagrammatic representation of this process):

1. The United States and Russia, in line with their legal commitment, should agree by 2007 on the counting rules for SORT, a schedule for arms reduction as called for under that agreement, and reliable verification and confidence-building measures. The duration of START I, with its system of verification and confidence-building measures, should be extended to 2012, and that of SORT until 2015, so that the term of implementation of arms reductions under SORT is not concurrent with the life of the treaty itself.

2. The exchange of full lists of data should be arranged concerning missile threats from other countries. Also, the

Joint Data Exchange Center in Moscow should be allowed to become operational in 2006, and with expanded functions.

3. Immediately upon finalizing work on SORT, the United States and Russia should initiate SORT II negotiations, with the purpose of reducing each state's arsenal of strategic nuclear arms to 1,000 to 1,200 warheads by 2017.

4. In 2006, Russia and the United States should begin talks on limiting and reducing their stockpiles of tactical nuclear weapons. Negotiating objectives should include these weapons' nondeployment in Central and Eastern Europe, their subsequent full withdrawal by the United States and Russia from Europe (i.e., the treaty zone as defined in the Conventional Armed Forces in Europe Adaptation Treaty), and their relocation to central storage facilities under mutual monitoring by 2012.

5. Russia and the United States should initiate the transition to a phased termination of the state of mutual nuclear deterrence between the two countries. They should begin by abandoning the operational concept of the launch-on-warning strike in 2006.

6. Corresponding with implementation of SORT, SORT II negotiations should get under way with the goal of a joint de-alerting of strategic nuclear forces by means of deactivation. The specific objective should be to reach an agreement by 2008 to verifiably de-alert all forces except 500 combat-ready warheads by 2012 (phase I), then going down to just 200 warheads by 2015 (phase II). These steps would be followed by de-alerting of 90 to 95 percent of strategic nuclear forces by 2020.

7. Along with the de-alerting process, there should be a joint understanding on limiting the number of ballistic missile nuclear submarines on sea patrol (this would primarily affect U.S. boats), on basing strategic bombers separately from nuclear bombs and air-launched cruise missiles, and on limiting the share of mobile ICBMs in land patrol areas (this would affect only Russian missiles).

8. The United States and Russia should complete organizational and technical integration of their missile early warning and reconnaissance systems by 2012, and interfacing of their command-and-control systems by 2017.

9. A full-scale treaty between Russia and the United States on cooperation in the development and deployment of the BMD system should be concluded in 2007, leading to its joint operational commissioning by 2020.

In a multilateral context, the following nine steps should be taken (as shown in Appendix A, these would occur concurrently with the bilateral U.S.-Russian agreements):

1. The United States and Russia should make a commitment in 2006, followed by Britain, France, and China, to foreswear first use of nuclear weapons against any Nuclear Non-Proliferation Treaty signatory, and to foreswear first use of WMD against any state (including Israel, India, and Pakistan, provided that they also adopt nuclear or WMD non–first-use doctrines).

2. The Comprehensive Test Ban Treaty should be ratified by all states (foremost the United States and China), and should enter into force in 2007.

3. Accelerated negotiations should occur toward conclusion of the Fissile Material Cut-off Treaty. The due verification provisions, with phase one dealing with uranium enrichment, should be in place by 2008.

4. The comprehensive Fissile Material Cut-off Treaty should be in place by 2010. It should include items addressing the separation of plutonium; full, verifiable accounting for all stocks of weapons-grade fissile materials; and the use of fissile materials for both peaceful purposes and legitimate military purposes.

5. A multilateral dialogue should be started in 2007 to involve Britain, France, and China in a regime of verification and confidence-building measures, and eventually should develop into agreements on nuclear arms limitations.

6. Starting in 2007, the Big Five nuclear states should begin a five-year effort to reduce conceptual reliance on nuclear deterrence in their national security strategies.

7. So-called third nuclear weapon states should be involved in de-alerting and deactivation procedures starting in 2012.

8. Starting in 2015, the cooperative missile early warning and monitoring regime should be extended to third nuclear weapon states that have joined the de-alerting regime, and to all states that join the missile launch notification regime.

9. Once the cooperative BMD protection system is put in place, in 2020, it should be extended to all states that have joined nuclear arms de-alerting agreements, cooperative missile early warning and monitoring arrangements, and launch notification mechanisms, as well as the regimes of the Nuclear Non-Proliferation Treaty, the Nuclear Suppliers Group, the Comprehensive Test Ban Treaty, the Missile Technology Control Regime, and the Fissile Material Cut-off Treaty.

These proposals for bilateral and multilateral action may, at first glance, look more like a wish list than a realistic program of action. It is true that the present policies of the U.S. and Russian governments, as well as those of Britain, France, and China, do not seem very encouraging. Besides, political tensions between Moscow and Washington, between Russia and the West, and between China and the West are rising on a number of international and domestic political issues.

A unique opportunity for such steps was missed during the mid-to-late 1990s. This was a blunder of historic scale, and its consequences are now noticeable in the political and strategic relations of the great powers. If, however, the growing strategic and political tensions draw attention back to nuclear weapons and nuclear deterrence, and provide incentives for realistic steps to deal with these problems, then there is still time to solve them, as long as the Cold War is kept firmly in the past.

As experience has demonstrated, neither high political tensions, like those of the Cold War, nor too deep a relaxation of political tensions, as occurred during the 1990s, is conducive to taking serious steps to do away with mutual nuclear deterrence. Hence, if it is at all feasible, now may be exactly the right time, if the political elites of the leading nations realize the need and understand the methods to achieve this objective.

After all, there are no insurmountable technical, economic, or strategic obstacles to doing away with mutual nuclear deterrence. The main barriers are in the minds of politicians, military leaders, weapons designers, and weapons producers. Changing the minds of as many of these people as possible, as well as the opinions of the general public and their political representatives, may provide yet another opportunity to do the job.

Appendixes

Appendix A
Assumptions in the Model Demonstrated by
Figures 5.1., 5.2, and 5.3

The full time it takes to reconstitute de-alerted missiles depends on the total number of SNF weapons at the given moment, the number of missiles and warheads remaining on full alert in each leg of the triad, and the methods of de-alerting, which determine the technical process of reconstitution.

Land-based ICBMs have the greatest launch-on-warning capabilities, and are the primary candidates in the strategic nuclear force for de-alerting. This is why in figures 5.1, 5.2, and 5.3 the model of de-alerting is illustrated by ICBM reconstitution time.

However, inasmuch as de-alerting is designed to achieve a much greater relaxation of strategic nuclear force postures and go much further toward transforming mutual nuclear deterrence relationships, abandoning launch on warning in favor of deep second-strike retaliation, SLBMs, and heavy bomber de-alerting would also be necessary. This is all the more so since with ever-fewer numbers of ICBMs on alert, land-based missiles would become increasingly vulnerable to attack by SLBMs if the latter were not de-alerted as well. This indirectly implies a considerable reduction in the number of ballistic missile nuclear submarines on sea patrol, since de-alerting of SLBMs is feasible only at submarine bases. This basing requirement would have the concurrent effect of reducing the number of SLBMs that could be launched from bases in a launch-on-warning first strike. (Firing of ballistic missiles from a submarine that is at its base is an accepted tactic in Russia, at least theoretically, and could be adopted in the future by the United States as well.)

The reconstitution time for SLBMs varies broadly, depending on the de-alerting method: from a few hours for each submarine in case of launch tube hatch welding to thirty days in case of the removal of missiles from launch tubes. Nonetheless, even with a limited number of installation and loading technical complexes at each base, SLBM reconstitution time (a maximum of 180 days for twelve ballistic missile nuclear submarines) would be covered by a significantly longer ICBM reconstitution process. Most probably the same is true for heavy bombers, even if their de-alerting is implemented through functionally related observable differences.

The full time for reconstitution of launch readiness of all ICBM forces depends on (a) the overall number of ICBM warheads in a de-alerted state, (b) the distribution of these warheads among missile bases and separate missile regiments (divisions), (c) the distance from the central base to each launcher, and (d) the capabilities of transportation and support technical personnel, among several other factors.

In figure 5.1, the modeling of the procedures of reconstitution of ICBM readiness for launch is done for Russia's ICBM force level in 2005.

In figure 5.2, the modeling is based on the same general assumptions for the reduced strategic nuclear force levels by 2012, when both sides would have about 2,000 warheads under SORT.

In figure 5.3, the model of reconstitution is based on the strategic nuclear force level of about 1,000 warheads we propose for attainment by 2017.

The dynamic models of reconstitution of the full readiness of strategic nuclear forces shows the maximum and minimum times (T max and T min), which correspond to various technical methods of de-alerting and de-activation of strategic forces.

Appendix B
A Proposed Sequence of Practical Bilateral and
Mulilateral Steps toward Ending Nuclear Deterrence

Year	Multilateral steps	Bilateral U.S.-Russian steps
2006	Non–first use of nuclear weapons	SORT finalized SORT extended to 2015 START I extended to 2012 Ban on launch-on-warning Launch of Joint Data Exchange Center
2007	Comprehensive Test Ban Treaty "Third" nuclear weapon states join arms control	Common BMD treaty
2008	Fissile Material Cut-off Treaty concluded	
2009		
2010	Fissile Materials Cut-off Treaty takes effect	
2011		
2012	Third nuclear states join de-alerting	Integration of ballistic missile early warning systems De-alerting to 500 combat-ready warheads each Withdrawal of tactical nuclear weapons to central storage
2013		
2014		
2015	Third nuclear states join common ballistic missile early warning system	De-alerting to 200 combat-ready warheads each
2016		
2017		Interfacing command, control, and communication systems SORT II (reduction to 1,000 to 1,200 total warheads each)
2018		
2019		
2020	Nuclear weapon states join common BMD	De-alerting to 100 combat-ready warheads each Deployment of common BMD

Notes. SORT, Strategic Offensive Reduction Treaty. START, Strategic Arms Reduction Treaty. BMD, ballistic missile defense.

Index

phased readiness reductions, 136–
40
See also specific nations
nuclear deterrence, 2–12, 163–70
ambiguities of, 30–36
contradictions. *See* paradoxes of
deterrence
cost considerations, 9–10
enhanced deterrence, 30–34
extended deterrence, 34–36
historic overview. *See* historic
overview of deterrence
limitations on cooperation, 8–9
political role, 16–38
in the post-Cold War era, 89–92
pragmatic approach, 54
reasons for, 5, 7–10
relevance to current situation, 7,
93–96
See also proposals for moving beyond deterrence
nuclear disarmament, 5–6, 14–16, 165
nuclear materials
Cooperative Threat Reduction
Program, 96–98, 100–101
Global Partnership anti-prolifera-
tion program, 96, 98, 100–101
nuclear minicharges. *See* bunker-
buster missiles
Nuclear Non-Proliferation Treaty, 7,
54–56, 142, 155, 169
Bush (George W.) administration
policies, 4, 70
first-use policies, 168
new nuclear states, 161–62
North Korea's withdrawal, 52–53
Nuclear Suppliers Group, 162, 169
nuclear threshold, 6
Nunn-Lugar Cooperative Threat Reduction Program, 96–98, 100–101

*On the Foundations of Strategic Relations
Between the United States of America
and the Russian Federation*, 151

Pakistan's security policies
ballistic missile defense (BMD)
systems, 154–55
mutual existential deterrence
against India, 46–47
potential for cooperation agreements, 161–62
war on terror partnership with
U.S., 9

weapons arsenal, 161
Panofsky, Wolfgang, 17–18
paradoxes of deterrence, 5–7, 13–56
bilateral deterrence relationships
matrix, 48, 49f
consequences of weapons use, 38–
39
cooperative weapons-reduction
programs, 96–101
Hegelian dialectic analysis, 54–55
leadership control scenarios, 39–
43
mutual deterrence, 43–50
political role of deterrence, 16–36
prevention of war, 49–51
"rational" views of deterrence, 36–
43
tactical weapons, 28–29
terrorist contexts, 51–56
Partial Test Ban Treaty of 1963, 55
partnership options. *See* proposals for
moving beyond deterrence
Peacekeeper MX missiles, 65, 70, 100,
128
People's Republic of China. *See*
China's security policies
phased readiness reductions, 126–40,
137t
asymmetric triads, 127–31
command-and-control systems,
136
early warning systems, 136, 142–
50
mutual second-strike capabilities,
128–29, 141
reconstitution time, 131, 132f, 133,
134–35f, 173–74
tactical nuclear weapons, 138–39
third nuclear states, 136–38
political reforms in Russia, viii, 3, 10,
96–101
political role of deterrence, 16–38
post-Cold War era, 6–7, 13–14, 89–104,
164
arms control policies, 93–96
Cooperative Threat Reduction
Program, 96–98, 100–101
Global Partnership anti-WMD
proliferation program, 96, 98,
100–101
phasing out deterrence, 101–3
treaty obligations, 95–96
power supply unit disassembly, 116–
17

About the Authors

Alexei Arbatov is a corresponding member of the Russian Academy of Sciences, where he serves as director of the Center for International Security, Institute for World Economy and International Relations. He is also a scholar in residence at the Carnegie Moscow Center. From 1993 to 2003, he served as deputy chair of the defense committee of the Russian parliament, the State Duma. In 1990 he was a member of the Soviet delegation to the START I talks.

Vladimir Dvorkin served with the Strategic Rocket Forces of the Russian Federation, retiring as a major general. He is a senior researcher at the Center for International Security, Institute for World Economy and International Relations. He formerly directed the Fourth Central Scientific Research Institute of the Ministry of Defense of the Russian Federation.

Vladimir Evseev served with the Strategic Rocket Forces of the Russian Federation, retiring as a lieutenant colonel. He is a senior researcher at the Center for International Security, Institute for World Economy and International Relations. He formerly served as chief of meteorological services of the ICBM Division of the Strategic Rocket Forces.

John D. Steinbruner is professor of public policy at the School of Public Affairs at the University of Maryland and director of the Center for International and Security Studies at Maryland (CISSM). His work has focused on issues of international security and related problems of international policy. He is currently vice-chair of the Committee on International Security Studies of the American Academy of Arts and Sciences and chairman of the board of the Arms Control Association.